F-14 A & B
TOMCAT

in detail & scale

Bert Kinzey

Airlife Publishing Ltd.

England

CONTRIBUTORS:

Lt. Larry Muczynski	Mike Campbell
Ray Leader	Warren Munkasy
Don Linn	Hugh Alcock
Ron Thurlow	George Cockle
VF-41	Grumman
Hughes	The U.S. Navy

Detail & Scale would like to express a special thanks to LTJG Mark Clemente of VF-41 for his assistance in supplying many of the photographs of the two Tomcats involved in the Libyan incident. A very special thanks is due Lt. Larry Muczynski, one of the pilots who shot down the Libyan Su-22s, for his time and efforts in writing his account of the incident for this book.

Most photographs in this book are credited to their contributors. Photos with no credit indicated were taken by the author.

FIRST EDITION
SEVENTH PRINTING

Cataloging-in-Publication Data

Kinzey, Bert
    F-14 A & B Tomcat : in detail & scale / by Bert Kinzey.
        p.   cm. -- (D&S ; vol. 9)
    Originally published Blue Ridge Summit, PA : TAB Books ;
Shrewsbury, England : Airlife, c1982.
    ISBN 0-89024-165-1 : $11.95
        1. Tomcat (Jet fighter plane) I. Title. II. Title: F-14 A and B
Tomcat.
[UG1242.F528 1993]
623.74'64--dc20   93-20523
                                           CIP

Published in Great Britain by
Airlife Publishing Ltd.
7 St. John's Hill
Shrewsbury, SY1 1JE

British Library Cataloging in
Publication Data

Kinzey, Bert.
F-14 A & B Tomcat in detail and scale
1 Tomcat (Jet Fighter Plane)
1 Title
623.74'64   TL686.G78
ISBN 0-85368-511-8

Front cover: In-flight photograph of an F-14 armed with six Phoenix missiles.   *(Grumman)*

Rear cover: F-14A with a Phoenix missile. The open radome and access panels show the colors of the radar antenna and associated equipment. Note also the colors of the inert Phoenix missile.   *(Hughes)*

INTRODUCTION

Head-on view of an F-14. Note the outward slant of the intakes.   **(Munkasy)**

Detail & Scale first published The F-14 Tomcat in Detail & Scale in early 1979. The entire print run was quickly sold out. Plans were made to reprint the book, but before these plans were put into action, talks began with Aero Publishers for them to take over publication and distribution of the Detail & Scale series while we at Detail & Scale concentrated on the development of the books. This arrangement resulted in a larger format with better printing than was available before.

Once the arrangement with Aero Publishers was finalized, consideration was given to revising and expanding our original publications into the new format. The sold out F-14 book was first on the list for this revision, and this publication is the result of that revision and expansion.

Readers who own the first F-14 book, which has now become a collector's item, will quickly see that this book is almost a completely new publication with many new features. Most noticeable of these new features is an account of the F-14's first use in combat in the downing of two Libyan Su-22s over the Gulf of Sidra. Detail & Scale has been fortunate in getting Lt. Larry Muczynski, one of the pilots who downed the Su-22s, to write, in his own words, his account of the Libyan incident. Readers will find this section of the book both enlightening and interesting.

Other new features of this book include coverage of the TARPS reconnaissance pod, more coverage of F-14 weapons, color photos of the open cannon bay, more cockpit photos, and an update of the new models that have appeared since the first book was released.

In general, this new release contains more coverage of all of the F-14 details. General details are shown in a "walk-around," while specific coverage is given to the landing gear, intakes, external fuel tanks, engines, glove vanes, tail hook, ejection seats, cockpits, cannon, and armament. Five-view 1/72nd scale drawings are also included.

At the time of this writing, the U.S. Navy is looking to improved versions of the F-14 which have been designated F-14C and F-14D. As these versions are developed and enter operational service, they will undoubtedly become prime candidates for another Detail & Scale volume.

It is the aim of the Detail & Scale series to present each aircraft in the most complete detail possible. On the pages that follow, we believe we have accomplished this goal with the F-14 Tomcat.

HISTORICAL SUMMARY

F-14, 160676, of VF-111, "Sundowners," in a subdued all gray scheme. When VF-111 went to an all gray scheme they changed the mouth and eyes to a more ferocious look than was on their aircraft before the changeover.
(Cockle)

During World War II the U.S. Navy established command of the seas through its use of fleets built around the aircraft carrier. Before the end of that war, the American fleet was to withstand attacks by Japanese airpower to include suicide attacks by conventional aircraft and even piloted rocket powered aircraft that were in actuality "human guided" missiles.

Although many U.S. ships were damaged and some lost to enemy action, the center of the fleet, the aircraft carrier itself, survived well. Not one Essex class carrier was sunk during the war, and, after the loss of the first U.S.S. Hornet in October 1942, no fleet carrier was lost. The U.S.S. Princeton, a light carrier, was the only aircraft carrier larger than the escort carrier classes to be sunk after 1942. While many carriers received substantial damage, this survivability is quite remarkable, and can be attributed to several factors. These include excellent construction, good fire fighting systems, the best fire control systems in the world controlling massive arrays of weapons, and the heroic actions of crews. But another important factor was that, in many cases, most of the attacking Japanese aircraft never made it to their targets, because they were intercepted by American fighters. More likely than not, the American fighter that made the interception was a Grumman product, the F6F Hellcat.

After the war, military aviation entered the jet age, and many things changed while others stayed the same. Planes got faster, and a new threat arrived on the scene. The Soviet Union began developing anti-shipping missiles that could be launched at their targets from bombers at "stand-off" ranges up to 200 miles. Other missiles could be launched from surface vessels at great ranges.

But the U.S. Navy still built its fleets around the aircraft carrier, and as the new super carriers arrived on the scene, new ways had to be found to protect them. One proposal was the Douglas F6D Missileer, a subsonic aircraft that bore a resemblance to that company's Skyknight. This aircraft was not designed to dogfight enemy aircraft, but instead, it was to carry eight XAAM M10 Eagle missiles. These long range missiles would be guided to their aerial targets, including aircraft and those long range missiles, by a radar carried in the F6D. But, as a single-mission aircraft, the Missileer fell victim of budget constraints, and the Navy was left wanting for a fleet defense fighter.

A year later, in 1961, a new Secretary of Defense by the name of Robert S. McNamara, thought that the TFX fighter, then being studied by the Air Force, could be adapted for the fleet defense mission. This aircraft, which was to become the F-111, was opposed by the Navy from the very start. It was too big and heavy, and just not suited for carrier use. But it could carry the Phoenix missile, a new, long range air-to-air missile that would be effective against aircraft and missiles.

Grumman was selected as contractor for the Navy's version of the F-111, designated the F-111B, and like the Navy, Grumman realized that the F-111 airframe could not be suitably adapted for carrier use. They had another design in mind, but had to work on the F-111B for some time before even the politicians and bureaucrats realized it just would not work.

When Grumman finally began work on their own design, it was forced to compete in a VFX competition with the likes of General Dynamics, McDonnell Douglas, LTV, and North American Rockwell. The VFX program called for an aircraft that would have a crew of two, two Pratt & Whitney TF30 engines, and would carry the Hughes AWG-9/Phoenix weapons system in addition to Sparrow and Sidewinder missiles and an internal cannon. Its mission would be to defend the fleet against hostile aircraft and missiles, the same as for the F6D and F-111B.

In January 1969, Grumman won the competition, and was awarded the contract for the VFX, which was to become the F-14 Tomcat.

The F-14 shared a few common features with the aborted F-111B. Both aircraft had a crew of two, twin engines, the AWG-9/Phoenix system, and variable geometry wings. But the similarities stopped there. The performance of the F-14 was far superior when it came to performing the air-to-air mission. It was ideally suited for carrier use, being considerably lighter, and somewhat smaller than the F-111B. Yet the F-14 was still the largest carrier-based fighter ever built.

While the F-111 had early problems with its variable wing, the F-14's computer controlled wing worked well from the start. The wing box, which had experienced failures on the F-111, seemed almost indestructible on the F-14. After the first F-14 prototype crashed on its second flight, the wing box was dug out of the wreckage and found to be virtually intact. It was returned to Grumman where it was used as a test fixture.

It should be recalled that Grumman had previous experience with variable geometry wings, not only with the F-111B, but with one of its own designs, the XF10F Jaguar. While being the only Grumman "cat" never put into production, the Jaguar was a flying test bed from which much was learned. But by the time the F-14 arrived, a number of variable geometry aircraft were flying or were in the planning stages. The Soviets were adding this feature to follow-on versions of their Fitter series of aircraft, and were building the MiG-23 Flogger, the Su-24 Fencer, and the Backfire bomber - all with variable geometry wings.

In the United States, the Air Force version of the F-111 proved itself after problems were corrected, and variable geometry was designed into the B-1 bomber. Europe had its entry with the Panavia MRCA Tornado. But the F-14 offered a first. It was the first aircraft where control of the wings was completely automatic, being controlled by a computer in response to mach number and angle of attack.

But the Tomcat had a lot more going for it than just a variable geometry wing. Designed into it were features to make it competitive against any known or postulated threat through the year 2000. But as sophisticated as it was, it was a dream to fly. Pilots reported that its stability, spin resistance, and general flying qualities instilled confidence in young pilots, and that the Tomcat was a very forgiving aircraft. As it became operational, it was welcomed into Navy fighter squadrons. As did its ancestor, the Hellcat of World War II, the Grumman Tomcat now is a vital part of the protection for U.S. fleets which still center around the aircraft carrier. As the battle around the Falkland Islands proved, big ships without such protection are extremely vulnerable to attack by aircraft and cruise missiles. The Tomcat is the only fighter

This rare photograph shows the mock-up of Grumman's XF10F Jaguar. This aircraft had a variable geometry wing, and gave Grumman experience with this design feature. This photo shows the horizontal stabilizers in their original position on the fuselage. They were later moved to the top of the vertical tail. **(Grumman)**

F-14, 159635, of VF-24 as seen at Offutt AFB, Nebraska, June 11, 1982. Note the external fuel tanks under the fuselage.
(Cockle)

The remains of the F-14 that went off of the USS John F. Kennedy are retrieved from the depths.(US Navy)

capable of intercepting any airborne threat against the fleet ranging from those small cruise missiles to supersonic aircraft flying above 100,000 feet.

The only foreign country to operate the F-14 was Iran. Before the fall of the Shah, Iran purchased 80 F-14s, but they saw little service before the Shah was overthrown. Just what happened to these aircraft is not known, but fears were expressed that they might fall into Soviet hands. Manuals and documents containing classified information about the Tomcat were in Iran at the time of the takeover, and one wonders just what happened to them. But once America's most advanced aircraft was sold to a country that was supposedly an ally, the Carter Administration saw fit not to support that ally, if it ever could have in the first place, and left some of our most sophisticated weaponry open to possible compromise.

Should there be any doubt about America's concern about safeguarding the Tomcat and its secrets, one does not have to look further than the events of September 1976 when an F-14 rolled off of the deck of the USS John F. Kennedy. While an F-14 from VF-32, "Swordsmen" taxied across the deck, its engines roared out of control, and the aircraft plunged into 2000 feet of water while its crew ejected. Attached to the aircraft was a Phoenix missile.

It took a great deal of effort and money over a period of almost two months to locate and recover the Tomcat and the missile which had become separated from it. Special diving craft were called in as were German salvage ships. The operation was carried out under the watchful eye of a Soviet spy ship. During the recovery, there were some flustrations and problems. The aircraft was found, lost again, then found again. But after much difficulty, the Tomcat and the missile were successfully recovered. While it is undoubtedly true that one reason for making such an expensive and time-consuming attempt to recover the aircraft was to determine what had caused the accident in the first place, it is unquestionably true that the overriding concern was to prevent the aircraft and missile from falling into Soviet hands.

AN AIR FORCE TOMCAT?

In 1974, Air Force General Daniel "Chappie" James, then Commander of NORAD, took an orientation flight in the F-14. With the F-106 Delta Dart having been the primary interceptor since 1959, it was due a replacement, and the F-14 seemed the most logical answer. With its long-range radar and Phoenix missile, the Tomcat can cover more airspace faster and more effectively than any other fighter in the world. Since defending the United States against air attack is not like defending a point target such as an airfield, but is a question of defending a lot of airspace, the Tomcat is clearly the best selection.

For some time the Air Force had a study to select and develop an "advanced manned interceptor," but they have failed to come up with one. This is hard to believe, and quite alarming considering the growing bomber forces of the Soviet Union. The F-15 Eagle, excellent air superiority fighter that it is, cannot perform this job as effectively as the Tomcat. After buying the Navy's F-4 and A-7, intra-service rivalry and politics prevented the F-14's selection by the Air Force. It would be better if our armed forces realized that the United States is one country, and it would be better if they all worked together to defend it. While Secretary of Defense McNamara proved that "commonality" could not be forced to work, it seems that when any piece of equipment is already ideally suited for another service, that much money could be saved if there was cooperation among all concerned.

When the Shah was overthrown in Iran, "Aviation Week" reported that Saudi Arabia was concerned over the loss of Iran's F-14 buffer between them and the Soviet Union. The report stated that Saudi Arabia wanted to buy F-14s, rather than wait for forthcoming orders of F-15s. The report went on to say that the Air Force was opposed to Saudi Arabia buying the Navy plane, and wanted the Saudis to stay with the purchase of their aircraft. It stated that the Air Force thought that the F-14 was too sophisticated for the Saudis.

The reason for this "editorializing" is to point up some of the controversy and politics involved with new aircraft development and production. This "politicing" not only involves the sales to foreign countries, sometimes before all the needs of American units are filled, but also involves petty rivalry between our own branches of the armed services - all of which have the same job of protecting freedom.

Another political consideration came up during the development of the F-14. With the RA-5C Vigilante and RF-8 Crusader extended past reasonable operational life, a reconnaissance version of the F-14 was proposed and considered. Several options were studied. These included cameras and sensors being mounted in the nose in place of the cannon, and another option was that of a canoe-like pod being mounted under the fuselage. This was a similar arrangement to what had been on the RA-5C.

But budget constraints forced the Navy to decide whether it would buy fighters, reconnaissance aircraft, or attack aircraft. It decided on fighters, leaving a void where a replacement was needed for the reconnaissance aircraft. Even after this decision was made, the Navy was forced to reduce the number of F-14s procurred, and the Marines lost the F-14s they were scheduled to receive outright. The reconnaissance problem was relieved to some degree by the interim TARPS system (covered next), but eight years after the RF-14 program was dropped, there is no new dedicated reconnaissance aircraft committed for use by the Navy.

VF-124 F-14, 160652, in an all gray scheme, September 19, 1981. **(Cockle)**

The F-14B test aircraft was used to test the Pratt & Whitney F401 engine in the Tomcat. Plans now call for the F-14C and F-14D versions to be equipped with the General Electric F101 engine. **(US Navy)**

Politics of a different nature became part of the F-14 story in August 1981 when two Libyan Su-22s fired on two F-14s operating off of the USS Nimitz. In less than one minute, the two F-14s shot down the Su-22s, and the F-14 had logged its first test in combat. A full account of this engagement is given later in this book as told by one of the pilots involved. It has been reported that other American aircraft had been fired on by the Libyans in the past, but were not allowed to defend themselves. Under the Reagan Administration, this return of fire by American forces is an international political move that shows Libya and the world that the U.S. will no longer tolerate such attacks on its forces.

As this book goes to press, the F-14 has been in service ten years. It has been a short ten years, and the F-14 is still thought of as a "new" aircraft. When compared to the F-4, it is, and it certainly will be around for some time to come. Considering the controversy in its operational life to date, one wonders what is yet to come. It rose out of the controversy of the F-111B, and was involved in a highly controversial sale to Iran. It is undoubtedly the best aircraft for defense of the North American continent, but this is a role in which it probably will never be used. It was involved in the most dramatic military incident in which the United States has been involved since the end of the war in Vietnam.

One thing that is probably in the Tomcat's future is a new engine. The idea of putting a more powerful engine in the F-14 is not new. The F-14B test aircraft were fitted with the Pratt & Whitney F401 engine, and the results were quite favorable. However, the F-14B was not put into production. The F-14C is now scheduled for introduction into the service in FY 1984, and it will have the General Electric F101 engine. It will also have a programmable signal processor, added computer memory, a television camera system, and a new non-cooperative target identification system. Later, around 1987, the F-14D will follow the F-14C into service, and will have a digitized radar with additional modes. The avionics system will also be digitized, there will be a new computer, stores management system, and a digitial inertial navigation system. It will have a longer fuselage with greater internal fuel capacity.

In addition to improvements to the aircraft, the new version of the Phoenix, the AIM-54C will replace the -A version. It will have even more range, and will not require aircraft cooling.

At present, the F-14 production lines are scheduled to be open until 1995, and the Tomcat will certainly be in service for ten to fifteen years beyond that. So there is yet a long future for the Tomcat, and it is sure to be an eventful one. But whatever comes next for Grumman's ferocious feline, it is sure to carry on the proud tradition of defending the U.S. fleet as established in World War II by the F6F Hellcat, and by all the other family members of Grumman's fighting cats.

F-14 TARPS

In-flight shot of F-14, 160914, from VF-124 showing the TARPS pod under the fuselage. **(Linn)**

With the retirement of the RA-5C Vigilante from service, and the RF-8 Crusader now being used only in the Navy Reserve, the Navy has found itself lacking reconnaissance assets. It must rely on the Marine RF-4B, but that airframe and its systems are aging and in limited supply. No definite and long range answer has been found to fill this need.

The optimum airplane would be one that was built from the ground up as a reconnaissance aircraft, but the cost factors would prohibit this. The second choice is to convert an existing airframe to perform the recon mission, but in doing this you compromise the design in one way or another. Further complicating the picture is the Navy's limited assets. Limited deck space, limited personnel, and other limitations also prevent pursuing the optimum solutions. The result is a trade-off between getting a system that will do the job as effectively as possible, but that can "live" with the limitations imposed on it.

The TARPS (Tactical Airborne Reconnaissance Pod System) has been designed as an interim system to fill the gap left with the phase-out of the RA-5C and the over-extended RF-8. It will be used until a more permanent solution to fill the Navy's reconnaissance needs can be obtained. One such answer may possibly be the RF-18 Hornet, a program now under consideration. Earlier, a dedicated reconnaissance version of the Tomcat, the RF-14, had been dropped. It only reached the "paper airplane" stage in 1974.

TARPS was originally designed for the A-7 Corsair II, and was developed over a four year period. Six engineering and developmental pods were produced and tested. No major changes were required to carry the pod at supersonic speeds on the F-14 instead of the much slower A-7. Pilots report that there is no noticeable effect on the Tomcat's performance at all with the pod in place. There is a little more buffet at high speeds at a low altitude, but otherwise, crews cannot even tell it's there.

The pod is mounted on station five, which is one of the Phoenix stations. When in place, the station next to it also cannot be used. The control panel for the

Head-on view showing the TARPS pod from the front.

(Linn)

system is located in the aft cockpit on the left console.

Plans call for thirty-four F-14 TARPS aircraft, and they will be integrated into some existing F-14 squadrons. There are normally two F-14 squadrons on each carrier, but only one will have TARPS F-14s. The current plan calls for three aircraft and anywhere from three to five crews. These aircraft can be converted to perform the normal F-14 mission, but a standard F-14 cannot be converted to a TARPS aircraft.

The crews are trained with VF-124 at Mirimar NAS, as are the maintenance personnel. These are F-14 crews with an additional syllabus added at the end of the training for TARPS.

As originally planned, the interim operational period for the pod was to be three to five years. However, as yet there has been no long term answer found that will meet the Navy's reconnaissance needs. It is now expected that the TARPS system will be in use for a minimum of seven years, and possibly as long as ten or twelve years.

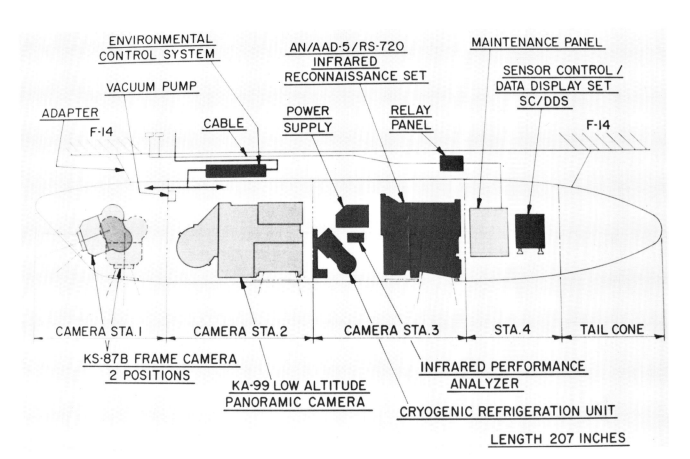

ENVIRONMENTAL CONTROL SYSTEM

VACUUM PUMP

ADAPTER F-14

CABLE

POWER SUPPLY

AN/AAD-5/RS-720 INFRARED RECONNAISSANCE SET

RELAY PANEL

MAINTENANCE PANEL

SENSOR CONTROL / DATA DISPLAY SET SC/DDS

F-14

CAMERA STA. 1   CAMERA STA. 2   CAMERA STA. 3   STA. 4   TAIL CONE

KS-87B FRAME CAMERA
2 POSITIONS

KA-99 LOW ALTITUDE
PANORAMIC CAMERA

INFRARED PERFORMANCE
ANALYZER

CRYOGENIC REFRIGERATION UNIT

LENGTH 207 INCHES

TARPS MAJOR SUBSYSTEMS

Nomenclature	Designation	Part Number	Manufacturer
(1) Pod Structure	LA-610	816-0611	NADC
(2) Serial Frame Camera	KS-87B	7320-1000-1	CAI
(3) Panoramic Camera	KA-99A	1264A5	Fairchild Camera
(4) Infrared Line Scanner	AN/AAD-5	YK15B2	Honeywell
(5) Control Indicator, Power Distribution Unit	C10491/A	816-1220	NADC
(6) Data Display Set	AN/ASQ-172	277-7000	Fairchild Space/Elec.
(7) Control, Processor, Signal	C10442/A	A51J12016	Grumman Aircraft Co.
(8) Environmental Control System	N/A		Grumman Aircraft Co.

(Courtesy of the U.S. Navy)

Close-up in-flight view of the TARPS pod from behind and slightly to the right. **(Linn)**

SUBSYSTEM DESCRIPTION

LA-610 TARPS POD

The pod structure is a compartmentized shell providing protective containment and mounting for three reconnaissance sensors with ancillary equipment. The pod is 207.5 inches long with a maximum cross-section of 26.5 inches and consists of the Nose Section, Center Section, Aft Section, Cable/Wiring, and Adapter.

KS-87B FRAME CAMERA

The Serial Frame Camera consists of the following major assemblies: camera body, magazine assembly, cassette assembly, light sensor, and 6 inch lens cone. The KS-87 frame camera is mounted in bay 1 so that it can be directed either forward to obtain photographs of the area seen by the pilot, or pivoted to a vertical position during a mission for use as a back-up sensor in the case of a KA-99 panoramic camera failure. The camera position movement can be accomplished in flight.

The 77.6 pound KS-87B serial frame camera (with film) is a government inventory item manufactured by Chicago Aerial, Incorporated. It will accommodate 1000 feet of 2.5 mil thick, 5 inch roll film, and can record up to six 4.5 inch square frames per second for a total of 2400 exposures. Data annotation is printed using a standard CRT recording head assembly.

KA-99 PAN CAMERA

The KA-99 Camera System is a 9-inch focal length low-to-medium altitude aerial reconnaissance camera. It offers full horizon-to-horizon panoramic imagery over a broad velocity/altitude mission envelope. The 250 pound camera system consists of three WRAs, the camera body, the magazine assembly, and the camera electronic unit. All are packaged together as a single unit and installed in bay 2 of the pod. Interface of the adapter frame to the pod structure is two in-line pivot bearings, permitting pivoting of the camera system for replacement of the magazine assembly and camera electronic unit.

AN/AAD-5 IR LINE SCANNER

The infrared reconnaissance set provides a high resolution film record of terrain being traversed by the aircraft. Scanning optics receive energy from the area under surveillance and are focused onto two detector arrays enclosed in a vacuum sealed dewar. Electrical signals representing the scanned area are displayed on a cathode ray tube as video. The displayed video is reflected and focused onto film to provide a continuous strip image of the terrain.

AN/ASQ172 DATA DISPLAY SYSTEM

The DDS performs three basic TARPS functions; (1) It provides data annotation on the sensor film recordings with necessary information for future interpretation of the recorded intelligence data; (2) It supplies necessary control signals to the individual sensors; and (3) It provides the signal flow interface between the aircraft systems and the pod equipment.

CAMERA MOUNT ASSEMBLY

The KS-87 camera mount assembly holds the camera for taking pictures. The mount assembly provides the capability to move the camera in flight from the vertical position to the forward position and back to the vertical. The mount assembly is made up of mechanical components, one electrical motor, and two positioning limit switches.

ENVIRONMENTAL CONTROL SYSTEM

The environmental control system is required to supply conditioned air for pod cooling and heating, and defogging the camera windows. Cool air is provided by tapping into the aircraft ECS system and running a cooling air line to the adapter. The air provided to the adapter will be 40°F from sea level to 30,000 feet and zero degrees above 30,000 feet. Available flow rate can be as high as 19 pounds per minute for all flight conditions. The air is further conditioned in the adapter by the use of a water separator to remove approximately 75% of the moisture, then is heated by a heater as required to maintain a desired pod temperature. A pod temperature sensor sends a signal to a controller which in turn sends a signal to a modulating valve that regulates the air flow into the pod and a signal to turn the heater on and off. Conditioned air is routed into the pod in bay 1.

Air for defogging is supplied on demand. The defogging air is heated in the same manner as that for the pod compartment. A sensor that determines the window glass temperature and dew point on the glass sends a signal to the controller which in turn sends a signal to the defogging modulating valve that regulates air flow to the three pod windows and a signal to turn the heater on and off. There is a defogging shut-off valve that shuts off air to the windows when the cameras are operating.

C10491/A - CONTROL INDICATOR POWER DISTRIBUTION UNIT

The CIPDU consists of a sensor test module, three sensor control modules, an aircraft simulator module, and printed circuit boards. The maintenance panel located in bay 4 provides manually resettable fail indicators for each of the various pod sensors and major pod equipment to guide maintenance personnel in the identification of faulty WRAs. The panel provides the capability of initiating and monitoring the BIT functions within the pod and a means of operating the sensors, individually or together, as a verification of proper operation following corrective maintenance or for pre-flight check out purposes. All pod equipment circuit breakers are located on the maintenance panel. An aircraft simulation unit is provided so that the pod equipment can be functionally checked without the aircraft computer operating.

C10442/A - CONTROL PROCESSOR SIGNAL

The control panel is located in the aft cockpit left console. The panel is the primary electrical interface between the pod and the F-14 aircraft with the capability to control all sensors. Also, the panel indicates when a sensor is operating, film remaining, and failure of the respective sensor, camera mount, and environmental control system.

(Component description courtesy of the U.S. Navy)

Close-up of the pod from the front showing the mounting pylon.

(Linn)

F-14 WALK-AROUND

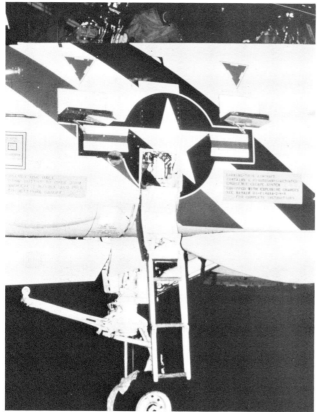

Above left: Nose of an F-14 from VX-4 showing the original IR/TV optical unit under the nose. The ALQ-100 antenna is mounted beneath the optical unit.

Above right: Nose with the ALQ-100 antenna and no optical unit. This is the arrangement on most F-14s.
                                                              (Munkasy)

Left: Close-up of the boarding ladder and steps on the left side of an F-14.   *(via Boll)*

Below left: Close-up of the wing leading edge at the hinge point.

Below right: Left wing tip detail showing position and formation lights.

Above left: Left rear fuselage area showing the left ventral fin. Note the oil cooler scoop which is located only on the left side of each fin.

Above right: Vertical tails from the left. Note the differences in the tips of the fins.

Right: Inside of right engine nacelle showing the oil cooler scoop on the inside of the right fin, and another scoop on the nacelle itself.

Below left: Chaff/flare dispenser just to the left of the arresting hook. This dispenser is sometimes covered.

Below right: Rear end view showing one engine nozzle closed, and one open.

Above left: Right rear ventral fin from the right. Note the lack of an oil cooler scoop on this side.

Above right: Underside of the right wing root. The dirty gray area on the fuselage just under the wing is an inflatable seal that expands as the wing moves forward. This fills in the area on top of the fuselage occupied by the wing when the wing is in the swept position.

Left: Canopy rail detail showing the series of hooks that latch the canopy down. The inside of the canopy rail is flat black.

Below left: A ground crewman services the liquid oxygen containers located in the right side of the nose. (U.S. Navy)

Below right: Right side of the nose showing the ground refueling connection.

Above left: Crewmen work on the direct feed unit in the spine of an F-14. (U.S. Navy)

Right: The spine of an F-14 with panels removed. (U.S. Navy)

Below left and right: Two views of the wing fold mechanism carapace structure. Above each structure are two stiffeners which also serve as upper-surface fences. In the right photo the air inlet bleed door is visible in the open position. (Alcock)

NOSE LANDING GEAR

Front view of the nose landing gear. Note how far apart the wheels are. Visible in this view is the box with the three approach indicator lights and the landing/taxi light above it. Also note the door hinges and retraction links.

Nose gear from the left showing the wheel detail and the catapult launch arm. The cylinder attached to the side of the strut is the nose wheel steering cylinder. (Cockle)

Nose gear doors from the left. Note the angle of the doors to one another in this view, and the small oval vent on the larger door. Door edges are in red with the insides white. The black area on the door is used for writing event number and gross weight information for the crew before each flight.

Nose gear from the right and behind. This view shows the retraction jack to the rear of the strut. The jack also serves as a brace allowing the nose gear to be used in catapult launches, thus eliminating the need for bridles and braces as used with the F-4 Phantom. Note the angle of the nose gear doors.

Above left: Nose gear well looking to the rear.

Above right: Nose gear well looking forward.

Below left. Nose gear attached to a catapult. Note how the strut is fully compressed when attached to the catapult.   *(Alcock)*

Below right: Looking straight up into the nose gear well. Forward is to the top of the photo.

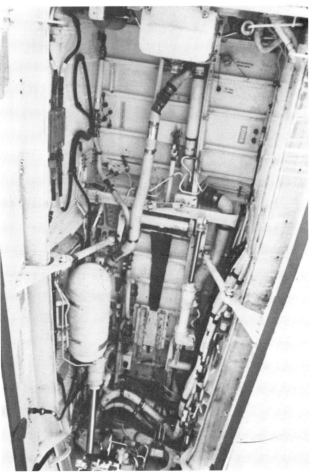

RIGHT MAIN LANDING GEAR

Right main landing gear from behind and to the right. Note the angle of the rear door.

Interior of the right main gear well looking up and in toward the fuselage. Note the actuating cylinder for opening and closing the inner door.

Right main gear well looking aft.

Right main gear well looking forward. Note the hinges on the forward outer door.

Right main gear wheel detail.

Inner view of the right main gear wheel showing the hydraulic lines and part of the brake assembly.

Above left: Side view of the left main landing gear.

Above right: Looking aft into the left gear well. Again note the angle of the rear door when open.

Below left. Inside view of the left main gear wheel.

Below right: Looking up into the left gear well showing the arrangement of all three doors.

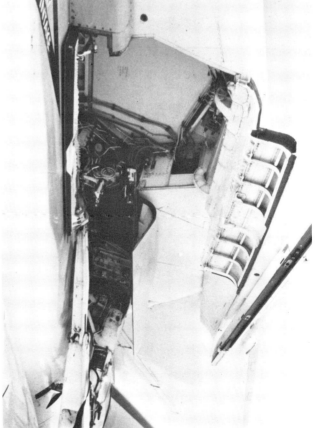

INTAKE DETAIL

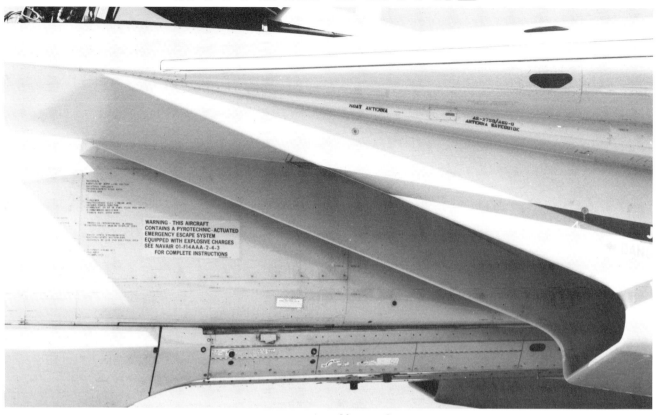

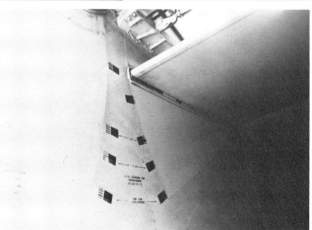

Above: General side view of the left air intake. Note that on this all gray aircraft the lower lip of the intake is painted gray rather than being natural metal as on the gray over white aircraft. (Cockle)

Left: Markings on the inner wall of the left intake. The slightly worn areas on the wall show the degree of movement of the ramps.

Below left: Looking down the intake showing part of the mechanism that operates the upper ramps.

Below right: Looking up into the intake and through the bleed air door in the top of the fuselage.

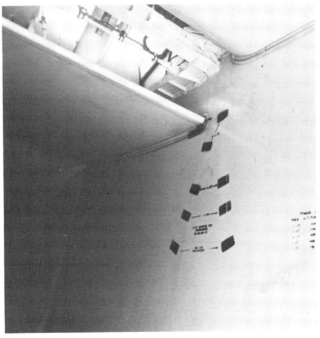

Above left: Right intake from the front with the FOD cover in place. Evidently it doesn't really matter which way is up!

Above right: The lower lip of the intake on aircraft painted in the gray over white scheme was usually left bare metal.

Right: Inner wall of the right intake with the ramps in the up position.

Below left: Bleed air doors on top of the fuselage in the open position.   *(via Boll)*

Below right: Right intake with the ramps in the lower position.

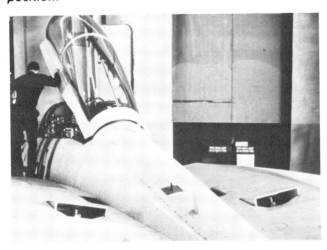

EXTERNAL FUEL TANKS & PYLONS

Above left: Left pylon without the fuel tank attached.

Above right: Right pylon attached under the intake.

Left: Left pylon with the external fuel tank attached.

Below left: Right fuel tank from the inside.

Below right: Right fuel tank from behind.

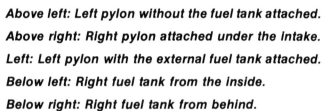

GLOVE VANES

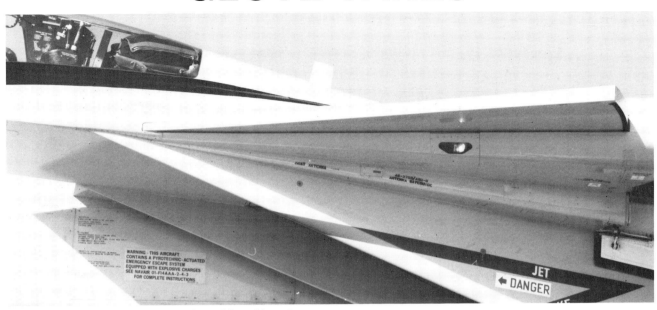

Left glove vane in the extended position. Note how thick the vane is. The glove vane is seldom seen in the extended position on the ground. *(Cockle)*

Right glove vane in the retracted position.

Another view of the left vane in the extended position as seen from underneath.

Left glove vane in the retracted position. Note the lights above and below the vane. *(Cockle)*

TAIL HOOK DETAIL

Above: Tail hook from the left.

Left: Rear portion of the tail hook as seen from the right.

Below left: Detail of the fairing and joint where the tail hook joins the fuselage. (Munkasy)

Below right: Tail hook from behind. Note the fuel dump located above the hook. (Munkasy)

ENGINE DETAIL

Above left: Engine bay on the right side open for servicing. (Alcock)

Above right: Forward panel on left side open showing engine detail. (Alcock)

Right: Engine details on the left side showing a mass of wires, lines, fittings, and related equipment. (via Boll)

Below left: Left engine bay with the engine removed. (Alcock)

Below right: Unusual photograph looking up the afterburner can.

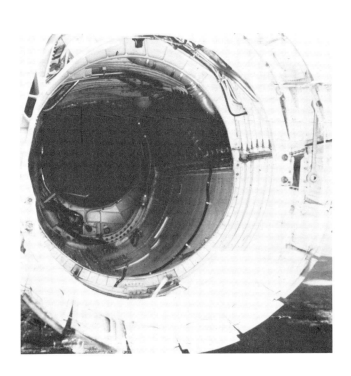

FLIGHT OPS AT SEA

A VF-14 "Top Hatters" Tomcat, shown at the instant of touchdown, is about to catch the wire on board the Kennedy.

Number 106 is shown on the flight deck with a Sparrow and a Sidewinder on the glove pylon. Note the subdued national insignia.

VF-14 Tomcat awaits its turn for launch from one of the waist catapults.

Aircraft 111 from VF-14 taxies forward after landing.

"Tomcat Alley." F-14s are shown parked on the USS John F. Kennedy while in port.

The CAG aircraft of VF-32 "Swordsmen" is shown being parked on board the USS Kennedy.

Another aircraft from VF-32 is brought to a stop after catching the wire.
All photos on these two pages are courtesy of Hugh Alcock.

F-14 COCKPIT LAYOUTS
FRONT COCKPIT

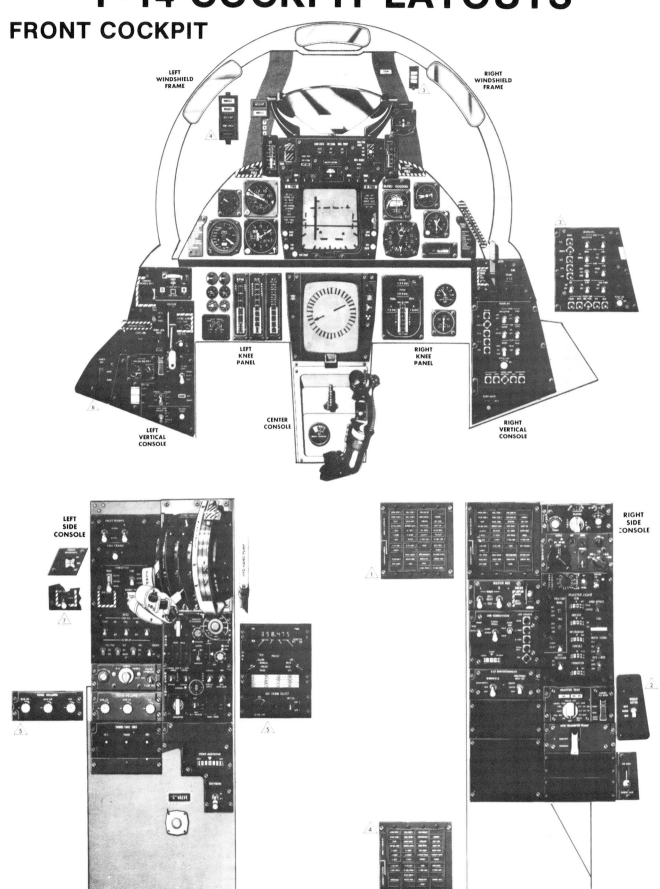

Courtesy of the US Navy

REAR COCKPIT

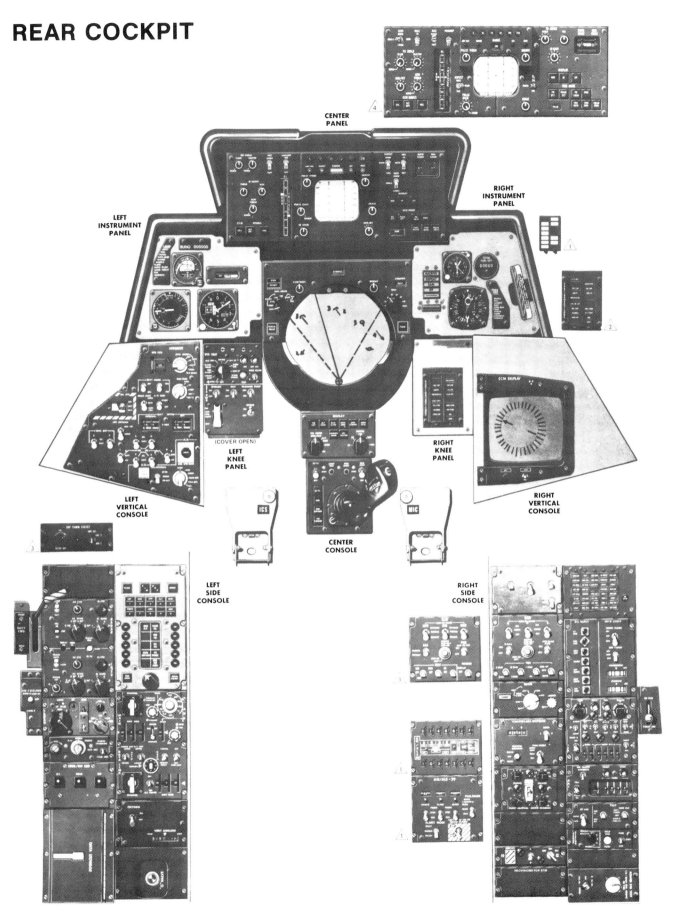

Courtesy of the US Navy

KEYS TO COCKPIT LAYOUTS

PILOT'S INSTRUMENT PANEL AND CONSOLES

NOTES

1. AIRCRAFT BUNO 158612 THRU 159001
2. AIRCRAFT BUNO 158631 AND SUBSEQUENT AND AIRCRAFT INCORPORATING AFC 35
3. AIRCRAFT BUNO 158978 AND SUBSEQUENT
4. AIRCRAFT BUNO 159002 AND SUBSEQUENT AND AIRCRAFT INCORPORATING AFC 181
5. AIRCRAFT BUNO 158978 AND SUBSEQUENT AND AIRCRAFT INCORPORATING AFC 599
6. AIRCRAFT BUNO 158987 AND SUBSEQUENT AND AIRCRAFT INCORPORATING AFC 529
7. AIRCRAFT BUNO 158978 AND SUBSEQUENT AND AIRCRAFT INCORPORATING AFC 334

LEFT SIDE CONSOLE
1. G VALVE PUSHBUTTON
2. OXYGEN VENT AIRFLOW CONTROL PANEL
3. COMM/NAV COMMAND CONTROL PANEL
4. INTEGRATED CONTROL PANEL
4a UHF (AN/ARC 159)
4b UHF COMM SELECT PANEL
5. TONE VOLUME CONTROL PANEL
6. ICS CONTROL PANEL
7. AFCS CONTROL PANEL
8. THROTTLE QUADRANT
9. INLET RAMPS/THROTTLE CONTROL PANEL
10. TARGET DESIGNATE SWITCH

LEFT VERTICAL CONSOLE
11. FUEL MANAGEMENT PANEL
12. CONTROL SURFACE POSITION INDICATOR
12a LAUNCH BAR ABORT
13. LANDING GEAR CONTROL PANEL
14. WHEELS FLAPS POSITION INDICATOR

LEFT KNEE PANEL
15. ENGINE PRESSURE RATIO INDICATOR
16. EXHAUST NOZZLE POSITION INDICATOR
17. OIL PRESSURE INDICATOR
18. HYDRAULIC PRESSURE INDICATOR
19. ELECTRICAL TACHOMETER INDICATOR (RPM)
20. THERMOCOUPLE TEMPERATURE INDICATOR (TIT)
21. RATE OF FLOW INDICATOR (FF)

LEFT INSTRUMENT PANEL
22. SERVOPNEUMATIC ALTIMETER
23. RADAR ALTIMETER
24. AIRSPEED MACH INDICATOR
25. VERTICAL VELOCITY INDICATOR
26. LEFT ENGINE FUEL SHUTOFF HANDLE
27. ANGLE OF ATTACK INDICATOR

LEFT FRONT WINDSHIELD FRAME
28. APPROACH INDEXER
29. WHEELS WARNING LIGHT
29a BRAKES
30. ACLS/AP WARNING LIGHT
30a NWS ENGA

CENTER PANEL
31. HEADS UP DISPLAY
32. AIR COMBAT MANEUVER PANEL
33. VERTICAL DISPLAY INDICATOR (VDI)
34. HORIZONTAL SITUATION DISPLAY INDICATOR (HSI)
35. PEDAL ADJUST HANDLE
36. BRAKE PRESSURE INDICATOR
37. CONTROL STICK

RIGHT FRONT WINDSHIELD FRAME
38. ECM WARNING LIGHTS
39. STANDBY COMPASS

RIGHT INSTRUMENT PANEL
40. WING SWEEP INDICATOR
41. RIGHT ENGINE FUEL SHUTOFF HANDLE
42. ACCELEROMETER
43. STANDBY ATTITUDE INDICATOR
44. CANOPY JETTISON HANDLE
45. CLOCK
46. BEARING DISTANCE HEADING INDICATOR (BDHI)
47. UHF REMOTE INDICATOR

RIGHT KNEE PANEL
48. FUEL QUANTITY INDICATOR
49. LIQUID OXYGEN QUANTITY INDICATOR
50. CABIN PRESSURE ALTIMETER

RIGHT VERTICAL CONSOLE
51. ARRESTING HOOK PANEL
52. DISPLAYS CONTROL PANEL
53. ELEVATION LEAD PANEL

RIGHT SIDE CONSOLE
54. COMPASS CONTROL PANEL
55. CAUTION–ADVISORY INDICATOR
56. TACAN CONTROL PANEL
57. MASTER GENERATOR CONTROL PANEL
58. ARA 63 CONTROL PANEL
59. AIR CONDITIONING CONTROL PANEL
60. MASTER LIGHT CONTROL PANEL
61. EXTERNAL ENVIRONMENTAL CONTROL PANEL
62. MASTER TEST PANEL
63. HYDRAULIC TRANSFER PUMP SWITCH
64. DEFOG CONTROL LEVER
65. WINDSHIELD DEFOG SWITCH
66. HYDRAULIC HAND PUMP

NFO INSTRUMENT PANEL AND CONSOLES

NOTES

1. AIRCRAFT BUNO 158978 AND SUBSEQUENT
2. AIRCRAFT BUNO 158612 AND SUBSEQUENT
3. AIRCRAFT BUNO 158978 AND SUBSEQUENT
4. AIRCRAFT BUNO 158978 AND SUBSEQUENT

LEFT SIDE CONSOLE
1. G VALVE PUSHBUTTON
2. OXYGEN VENT AIRFLOW CONTROL PANEL
3. COMM/NAV COMMAND PANEL
4. ICS CONTROL PANEL
5. INTEGRATED CONTROL PANEL
6. TACAN CONTROL PANEL
7. LIQUID COOLING CONTROL PANEL
8. COMPUTER ADDRESS PANEL
9. RADAR IR / TV CONTROL PANEL
9a UHF COMM SELECT PANEL
10. EJECT COMMAND PANEL

LEFT VERTICAL CONSOLE
11. ARMAMENT PANEL

LEFT KNEE PANEL
12. SYSTEM TEST — SYSTEM POWER PANEL

LEFT INSTRUMENT PANEL
13. SERVOPNEUMATIC ALTIMETER
14. AIRSPEED MACH INDICATOR
15. UHF REMOTE INDICATOR
16. STANDBY ATTITUDE INDICATOR

CENTER PANEL
17. DETAIL DATA DISPLAY PANEL (DDD)

CENTER CONSOLE
18. NAVIGATION CONTROL AND DATA READOUT
19. TACTICAL INFORMATION DISPLAY (TID)
20. TACTICAL INFORMATION CONTROL PANEL
21. HAND CONTROL UNIT

RIGHT INSTRUMENT PANEL
22. FUEL QUANTITY TOTALIZER
23. CLOCK
24. THREAT ADVISORY LIGHTS
25. CANOPY JETTISON HANDLE
26. BEARING DISTANCE HEADING INDICATOR (BDHI)

RIGHT KNEE PANEL
27. CAUTION ADVISORY PANEL

RIGHT VERTICAL CONSOLE
28. MULTIPLE DISPLAY INDICATOR

RIGHT SIDE CONSOLE
29. DIGITAL DATA INDICATOR (DDI)
30. ECM DISPLAY CONTROL PANEL
31. DATA LINK REPLY AND INTERIOR LIGHT CONTROL PANEL
32. ECM CONTROL PANEL
33. DECM CONTROL PANEL
34. DEFOG CONTROL LEVER
35. IFF TRANSPONDER CONTROL PANEL
36. CHAFF/FLARE DISPENSE PANEL
37. AA1 CONTROL PANEL
38. AN ALE 29A PROGRAMMER
39. IFF ANTENNA AND TEST PANEL
40. RADAR BEACON CONTROL PANEL
41. KY 28 CONTROL PANEL
42. ELECTRICAL POWER SYSTEM TEST PANEL

LEFT AND RIGHT FOOT WELLS
43. MIC FOOT BUTTON
44. ICS FOOT BUTTON

Courtesy of the US Navy

F-14 COLORS

F-14A of VF-1, "Wolfpack" in flight. This aircraft is painted in the gull gray over white scheme used prior to the introduction of the all gray scheme with more subdued markings.   *(U.S. Navy)*

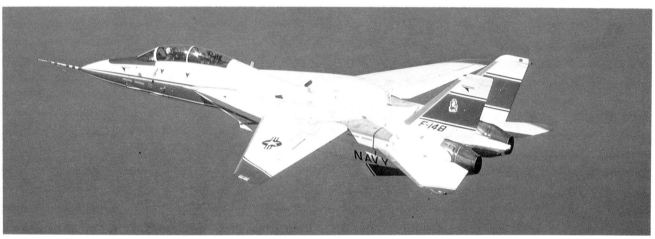

F-14B, in its colorful red and white scheme, photographed on a test flight. Note the Tomcat insignia on the tail.   *(Grumman)*

The only foreign nation to use the F-14 was Iran before the fall of the Shah. This Tomcat wears the distinctive Iranian camouflage, but retains U.S. markings prior to its departure from the United States.   *(Thurlow)*

F-14As from VF-32, "Swordsmen," off of the USS John F. Kennedy flying combat air patrol (CAP). Note the mix of AIM-9L Sidewinders, AIM-7 Sparrows, and AIM-54 Phoenix missiles. *(Alcock)*

VF-142 Tomcat from the USS America as photographed at Homestead AFB in November 1976. *(Munkasy)*

F-14, 161147, from VF-31 at NAS Oceana in May 1981. *(Alcock)*

Rear view of an F-14 from VF-1 awaiting a "lift" aboard the USS Enterprise. *(U.S. Navy)*

F-14A from VX-4, Operational Test and Evaluation Force, March 1977.

CAG CATS

CAG F-14 from VF-84, USS NIMITZ. VF-84 is known as the Jolly Rogers, and the squadron has a skull and crossbones on an all black tail. This has proved to be one of the most popular squadron insignias on F-14s. *(Huston)*

CAG aircraft from VF-2 from the USS Enterprise. This photograph was taken at Miramar NAS shortly after the changeover to the all gray scheme. *(Huston)*

VF-51 CAG aircraft at Miramar NAS in September 1978. For some time after the all gray scheme was introduced, national insignia and other markings remained large and colorful as they had been on the gray over white scheme. *(Huston)*

VF-143 CAG Tomcat from the USS America. VF-143 is the "Puckin Dogs," and this December 1976 photo shows the aircraft in the original gray and white scheme. *(Huston)*

Another popular scheme is that of VF-111, "Sundowners." Contributing to the popularity of the scheme are the mouth and eyes on the nose. This aircraft is from the USS Kitty Hawk, and careful examination of the rudder will reveal small stars in the different squadron colors. *(Huston)*

CAG F-14 from VF-11 photographed shortly after the squadron transitioned to F-14s. This photo was taken at NAS Oceana, and Don Shearer, a former Iranian hostage, had just been named CO of VF-11.

20MM CANNON DETAIL

Open panels show the ammunition drum located behind the boarding ladder and some of the "black boxes" on the Tomcat's left side.

Forward portion of cannon bay showing barrels, rotating assembly, and gun muzzles. (Grumman)

View of open cannon bay looking up and slightly forward. (Grumman)

FRONT COCKPIT DETAIL

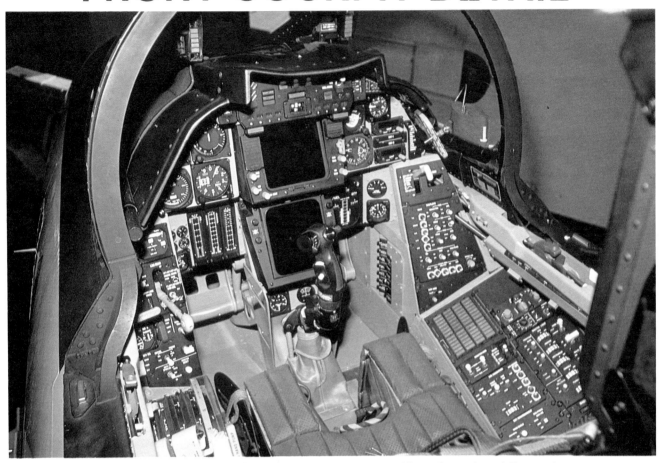

Front instrument panel and control column in the front cockpit. Note the color of the seat.

Left console in the front cockpit.

Right console detail in the front cockpit.

All photos on this page are courtesy of Grumman.

REAR COCKPIT DETAIL

Rear instrument panel detail.

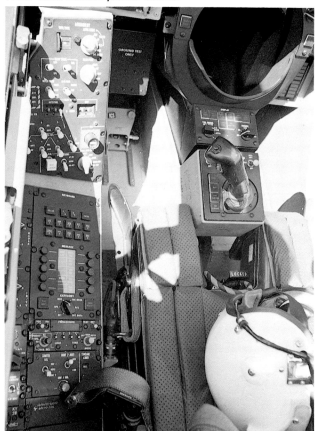

Left console detail in the rear cockpit.

Right console in the rear cockpit. (Alcock)

Another view of the NFO's instrument panel and radar control handle in the rear cockpit of an F-14A. (Hughes)

Ejection seat detail in the rear cockpit. *(Alcock)*

Circuit breaker panel on the right side of the seat in the rear cockpit. *(Alcock)*

Circuit breaker panel on the left side of the rear seat. *(Alcock)*

THE LIBYAN INCIDENT

Commander Kleemann's aircraft, 160403, as it appeared upon its return to Oceana. The kill marking is under the spade. By this time Lt. Venlet had left VF-41, and his name on the rear canopy rail has been replaced with that of LCdr Brian Felkema. At the time of the engagement this aircraft had the nose number 102, and "CDR MIKE FIELD" on the front canopy rails, and "LT STEVE WALKER" on the rear rails. (Campbell)

Lt. Larry Muczynski's aircraft, 160390, as seen right after the engagement on the USS NIMITZ. At this time the crew names had been painted on the canopy rails. They read, "LT MUCZYNSKI" in front, and "LT ANDERSON" on the rear. First names were not used. At this time, the kill marking was located under Lt. Muczynski's name on the left side. (VF-41)

160390 as it appeared on February 10, 1982 upon its return to NAS Oceana. At this time, the names on the canopy rails had been temporarily changed. They were later changed again to "LT LARRY MUCZYN-SKI" and "LT JIM ANDERSON," and other changes were also made. (Campbell)

160390 as it appeared on April 4, 1982. Note the marking changes. The E award has been added under the spade replacing the kill marking seen in the photo at left. The kill marking now appears under the canopy rail just forward of the front ejection seat warning triangle. (Campbell)

MARKINGS OF THE Su-22 KILLERS

The F-14 flown by Cdr. Hank Kleemann during the engagement as photographed shortly thereafter. The nose number has been changed from 102 to 101, and the kill marking has been added on the tail just under the spade.
(VF-41)

The markings carried by the two F-14s that downed the two Su-22s have been changed several times, and keeping them straight is somewhat complicated and difficult. After a great deal of research with VF-41, we have put together this explanation of these markings for the benefit of the marking enthusiast and the scale modeler.

VF-41's F-14s were painted in the overall gray scheme during the 1981 cruise aboard the USS Nimitz. Wheel wells and struts were white, as were the insides of the doors, with the edges of the doors painted red. The inside of the intakes were gray, and there was no bare metal on the leading edges of the flying surfaces. Instead, the light gull gray paint covered all leading edges.

Tail markings consisted of a dark gray spade with a white 41. A red band was placed diagonally on either side of the spade. A small AJ was at the outside bottom of each rudder, with the last two digits of the aircraft number at the top. The nose number was on each side of the nose, and was repeated on the flaps.

Cdr. Henry Kleemann, the squadron commander, was assigned to aircraft 101 as is the usual case with squadron commanders. (Numbers ending in 00 are reserved for the Commander of the Air Group). Cdr. Kleemann's NFO was Lt. Dave Venlet. The other crew, Lt. Larry Muczynski and Lt. Jim Anderson, were assigned to aircraft 112. However, crews rarely fly their own aircraft, and during the engagement Cdr. Kleemann flew 102 which was assigned to VF-41's XO, Cdr. Mike Field, and his NFO, Lt. Steve Walker. The BuNo. of this aircraft was 160403. Lt. Muczynski

and Lt. Anderson were in 107, BuNo. 160390, and according to VF-41's corrosion control people, there is no record of any crew names being on the aircraft at the time of the engagement.

After the engagement, the number on 160403 was changed to 101, thus making it the commander's aircraft. Cdr. Kleemann's name, and that of Lt. Venlet's, was painted on the canopy rails. The number of 160390 was left as 107, but Lt. Muczynski's and Lt. Anderson's names were added to the canopy rails, but only last names were used. Kill markings were originally added to both aircraft under the canopy rails on the left side, but this was later changed to a position under the spade on outer sides of both vertical tails. Later photographs, taken after the squadron returned to Oceana NAS, show the kill marking back under the canopy rail, and the "E" award painted under the spade. In his narrative on the engagement, Lt. Muczynski reports that the kill marking was again under the spade during a cruise on the USS Nimitz in July and August 1982. According to Lt. Mark Clemente, VF-41's Public Affairs Officer, the kill marking was an on again, off again situation for some time after the engagement.

When the squadron returned to Oceana in February 1982, Lt. Venlet had transferred out of the squadron. His name was removed from the rear canopy rails of 101, and was later replaced with that of LCdr. Brian Feikema.

Photos beginning on page 40, and included with Lt. Muczynski's report, show many of the markings carried on these two aircraft.

PILOT'S ACCOUNT

Lt. Muczynski's and Lt. Anderson's names as added to 107 shortly after the engagement. **(VF-41)**

Note: Although the engagement that resulted in the downing of the two Su-22s has been written up elsewhere, Detail & Scale was fortunate enough to get Lt. Larry Muczynski, one of the pilots who shot the Su-22s down, to give us an account of the engagement in his own words. He gave it to us on tape, and it is presented here practically word for word. His report is both interesting and informative, and although Detail & Scale does not usually use combat reports in our publications, we thought this account was worthy of exception. This was the first time the F-14 was ever used in combat, and this was the first air-to-air encounter in which all aircraft involved were variable geometry wing aircraft.

Lt. Muczynski is a 1976 graduate of the United States Naval Academy, and he received his Naval Aviator's wings in August 1978. He was assigned to VF-41 in July 1979, this being his first assignment in an operational squadron. In August 1982, he transferred out of VF-41 to shore duty as an instructor pilot.

Here is his account of the events leading up to the engagement, the engagement itself, and what hap-

pened immediately afterwards.

We left on cruise on August 3, 1981, and it took about a week to get over to the Mediterranean. There we met up with the USS Forrestal, which we were scheduled to relieve. We did a few days of work with the Forrestal, then moved down to the Gulf of Sidra area for the live missile shoot. This area is chosen because it is about the only place in the Mediterranean where there isn't much going on in the form of air or sea traffic. Warnings about the missile shoot were put out in Notices to Airmen (NOTAMS) and Notices to Mariners about one week before the shoot was to take place, and then about two days before. The missile shoot was scheduled to take place on August 18 and 19, 1981.

The place where the conflict comes in is that the Libyans, unlike most other nations of the world, claim about two or three hundred miles of internal waters, and international law says you can only claim about twelve or sixteen miles. So the United States does not recognize their claim, and neither does any other country, for that matter. Some of the area involved in the missile shoot, and put out in the Notices to Airmen and Mariners, hung down into what they claim is their internal waters. So there is where the possible area of conflict comes in. In years past the United States has gone down into that area, sent our P-3s and some surface vessels down there, and there has been assorted claims that we have been shot at, and they claim that they have shot at somebody. So there has been trouble in that area for several years.

When the Nimitz and the Forrestal pulled down there for the missile shoot, the stage was kind of set for a possible confrontation, but we, as aircrews, personally didn't think anything was going to happen as far as shooting or getting shot at was concerned. We knew there was a very good chance that we would

The loser. A Libyan Su-22 Fitter is shown here with an AA-2 Atoll missile under its wing. **(via Malerba)**

An AIM-9L Sidewinder on station 1A (one alpha). It was this type of missile fired from this station that was used by both F-14s to down the Su-22. (U.S. Navy)

see, intercept, and fly with and against some of the Libyan aircraft, and we were looking forward to that. It would be the first chance for most of us in the squadron to see Soviet-made aircraft, which is mostly what the Libyans have. They have the Mig-25 Foxbat, the MiG-23 Flogger, the MiG-21 Fishbed, the Su-22 Fitter, some French Mirage V's, and some assorted other aircraft.

The first day we went down there, which was the 18th of August, we went on CAP (combat air patrol) station at dawn and covered the area with seven CAP stations. The Nimitz was basically up to the north with two F-14 squadrons, and the Forrestal was on the eastern side with their F-4s. That morning we started seeing the Libyan sections come out, and they always flew in sections of two aircraft. We intercepted several of their sections, and some of them were very docile, and some were very aggressive in that they were always maneuvering for an offensive position. Of course we weren't going to allow that to happen, so we maneuvered as well. This made for the typical World War II type of dogfight where everybody is doing hard maneuvering, but no shots were fired. When everybody ran out of gas they would head home and we would return to the ship.

There was somewhere around thirty to thirty-five

sections intercepted on that first day. I got to intercept a section of two MiG-25 Foxbats, which is the first time anybody had ever seen any of those, especially myself. You always hear about how great an aircraft the MiG-25 is, but it really wasn't that much of a problem to get behind them and then stay offensive after that. It was a lot of fun! Several other sections saw MiG-23s, MiG-21s, and Mirage aircraft.

In debriefing that evening, we all got together and talked over what we had seen that day. We pretty much agreed that the Mirage drivers were the best of the bunch. They were the most aggressive; they knew how to use their aircraft the best. They made good use of the vertical, airspeed, altitude, and burner. The MiG-23 drivers were the worst of the bunch. They were not real aggressive, and would allow you to take pictures of them. Some were good, and some weren't so good, but that is true anywhere. You are going to have some good pilots and some poor pilots. The debriefing was quite casual, and was a "what did you see, what did I see" type of thing. There were not a whole lot of lessons to be learned.

The second morning we went out at dawn again. This was the launch where Cdr. Kleemann and myself went out. He initially was sent to a different station, and I came off the tanker and went to station four. Since I was on the way down there by myself, they told him to go down there with me, and sent someone else to take his place on the other station.

We arrived down there and went into an orbit pattern on CAP station. The day before, this station had only one intercept, so we were not real happy about being sent down there. In fact we were trying to think of ways to get off of that station and go someplace else. What we had determined was that once we got down to what we call our combat fuel load, we would call for relief on station, go back and hit the tanker, and then go to another station.

After about forty-five minutes on station, we determined we would have to stay there only a couple of more times around the race track pattern we were flying oriented north-south, and then we would be down to the fuel weight, call for relief, and then leave.

About that time we turned south one more time, and Dave Venlet, Commander Kleemann's radar officer, picked up a target coming out of the airfield we were watching in Libya. Shortly thereafter, my radar officer, Jim Anderson, picked up the same target. It immediately became obvious that they were coming towards us, because they were heading right at us and climbed to 20,000 feet which was our altitude. They accelerated up to 540 knots. Commander Kleemann was flying lead, and I was flying wingman on his three o'clock position, about a mile or two out

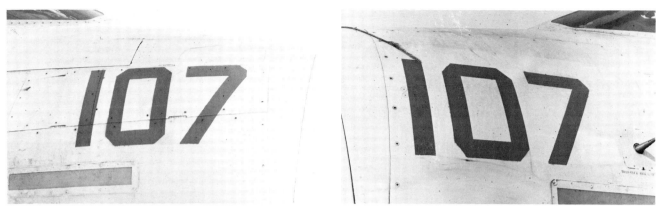

Nose numbers on 107. Note that the 7 is of a slightly different style on the right than on the left. Also note the yaw string in the right photo. **(VF-41)**

so it was easy to see him.

As we determined that the Libyan section was coming after us, we decided we had better get in a position to be offensive on them. I went into what we call an offensive combat spread. I went to about six to eight thousand feet above Commander Kleemann, and took about a two mile split on him. This puts me in a different plane than him, and makes it harder for the enemy aircraft to see me. We flew that formation down on the intercept run.

As we closed on the Libyans, we tried to take cuts on them to get lateral separation on them so as to make our turn in behind them easier. However it became obvious that they had good GCI (ground control intercept), in that every time we would take a cut, they would take a cut to neutralize what we had done. This made it impossible to get the initial advantage like we wanted to.

Finally, at about ten miles, it became obvious that nobody was going to get the initial advantage on anybody, so we just put them on the nose. Commander Kleemann, who was what we call the "eyeball," took them right down the nose to get a visual ID on them. I was the high wingman, what we call the "shooter," coming down with ninety degrees off, trying to get aspect on them right away and get behind them.

Commander Kleemann got a "tally ho" on the two aircraft at eight miles, and I got one about four miles as I was starting my turn in on them. I had wanted to be acute on Commander Kleemann, but because of the tremendous closure we had, we had to go to zone five afterburner to get our speed up to 500 knots. I didn't end up acute, in fact I ended up about his four o'clock position, a little bit sucked on him instead. This didn't turn out to be an all bad place to be.

When Commander Kleemann was 1000 feet in front of them and about 500 feet above them, he rolled his left wing down to pass directly above the section so he could get his visual ID on them. At that time, the left side of the lead Libyan aircraft lit up with a big flame as the missile motor ignited. I was on that side, so it was very obvious to me with a tremendous orange flash and smoke trail coming off the plane and going out under Commander Kleemann's plane. It then did sort of a banana up toward my plane, but it was also immediately obvious that neither one of us was going to get hit by the missile, so it didn't bother either of us. It immediately was no factor in the situation.

The Libyans were flying not in a combat spread nor a welded wing, but basically sort of a "lose duce" combat cruise, with about 500 feet horizontal separation on a line of bearing right. The wing aircraft was to the leader's right. When they fired they split, with the lead aircraft making a climbing left hand turn. The wing aircraft did a hard horizontal starboard turn back to a heading of 180. It looked like all he wanted to do was go back home.

At this time I was coming "down the hill," and was doing a hard turn closing in behind the leader. Commander Kleemann initially had also gone after the leader, but when he saw me closing on him, he reversed his turn back toward the wingman. I think it was a natural reaction for all of us to go for the guy who had shot at us.

Commander Kleemann got behind the wingman

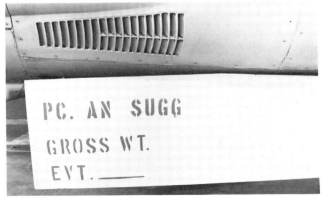

Marking on the left nose door on 107. **(VF-41)**

44

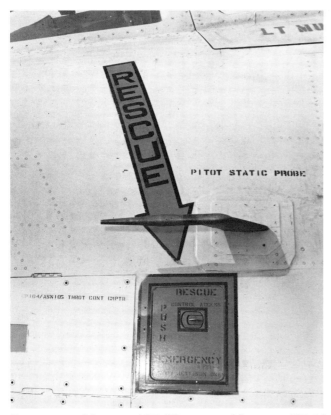

Rescue marking on 107. These markings on VF-41 Tomcats are different from those on many other F-14s in that the letters in the word "RESCUE" are vertical (one on top of another) rather than side by side. **(VF-41)**

Markings on the right vertical tail. Note the style of the 07 and the AJ. The spade is dark gray, not black. At the time this photograph was taken, the kill marking was located on the left side of the nose under Lt. Muczynski's name. **(VF-41)**

very quickly, but being early in the morning the sun was low on the horizon. The wingman, I believe by accident rather than design, happened to fly across the sun as he was making his hard starboard turn. So Commander Kleemann just waited on his shot for the guy to clear the sun.

The rules of engagement we were operating under at the time stated that we could fire, one, when the admiral came up with his code words and told us to engage a certain target, or two, if we were ever shot at. So we were operating under the rule of having been fired at, and both aircraft were immediately declared hostile by us, and we were free to engage them. We were expected to engage them.

As the wingman cleared the sun, Commander Kleemann was about forty degrees off the guy's tail, at about three-quarters of a mile. He fired an AIM-9L off of station 1A (left glove pylon, shoulder station). The missile pulled lead, then did a ninety degree reversal and hit the aircraft in the tail. Commander Kleemann and Lt. Venlet saw fragments come off of the aircraft, but they were not sure whether it was the warhead exploding or parts of the aircraft flying off. In any case, the results were the same. The aircraft started to roll, the drag chute deployed, and the guy imme-

diately ejected. He got a good chute and started down.

The leader, whom I had gone after, had completed his climbing turn, and was heading straight away north-northwest. He started a slight right hand reversal, but I had obtained a good firing position behind him. I armed up my AIM-9L, and also fired from station 1A. The Sidewinder went right up the guy's tail-pipe and blew off everything from the wing roots rearward in a tremendous fireball. Since I was only one-half mile at the guy's dead six, the thing that scared me the most was that I would shoot myself down because of the FOD going down the engines.

I did a 6 g pull-up, straight into the vertical, and when I cleared the debris pattern, I rolled inverted. I looked down and could see everything from the wings forward spinning on its way down and the plane on fire. After about two turns, I saw the pilot eject from the aircraft, but we did not see him get a good parachute. This is not to say that they do not have a barometric altimeter in their chutes set to open at ten or fifteen thousand feet like the United States does. We were at about twenty-thousand feet when the guy got shot down. At any rate, we did not see a chute at that time.

When that was over with, we called Commander Kleemann, and determined that, based on the separation the Libyans had taken, we were eight miles apart. I did a 360 degree turn, and Commander Kleemann came back to the north and we joined up. We then headed back to the Nimitz.

It wasn't until we were headed back to the Nimitz that we really had time to think about what had happened, and started calming ourselves down. The initial reaction when the missile had come off of the Libyan aircraft was just one of complete amazement and surprise. I don't think there was any fear on anyone's part, because there wasn't any time for it. We felt we had a job to do, so do it now. It wasn't upsetting, it was more reaction to the situation, and this is where the training and good equipment the United States give us pays off. I felt completely competent to do the job I was trained to do. Luckily it worked out well for both of us.

On the trip back to the ship we talked to everyone on the ship. All the fighters were up on a common frequency, so everybody could hear what was going on when we were making our calls during the engagement. The engagement, from the time the Libyans fired until the second guy was on the way down, only took forty-five seconds.

The captain of the Nimitz had announced to the crew that two F-14s had shot down two Libyan aircraft. So the mood on the ship was very excited.

When we finally did get back to the ship, Commander Kleemann came in to land first, and he had a bolter. (A bolter is when the aircraft misses all of the arresting cables, and has to go around for another landing.) This is unusual for him, because he is such a good solid pilot, and hardly ever bolters. He must have been pretty excited to do that. I was fortunate enough to get aboard on my first try. Commander Kleemann came back and boltered again on his second attempt. It is unheard of for him to bolter twice in a row. Then on his third attempt he got aboard with an OK three-wire trap.

By the time we taxied to our final spots on the carrier, everybody was milling around our aircraft. Our ordnance men had come over, and had taken the umbilical cords from where the "Winders" had been fired. They were holding them up for us, and later gave them to us as momentos of the day.

The line division had already heard about it, and had already come up with a silhouette of a Fitter. Instead of painting a Libyan flag on the aircraft, which is just a green rectangle and is pretty hard for the average person to recognize, our line guys wanted to put the silhouettes of Fitters on each aircraft.

As soon as we had the aircraft shut down, and were

getting out of them, they already had a can of spray paint and had painted the silhouette on the planes. They placed them right under the canopy rails. Commander Kleemann, the Skipper of the squadron, said that this was all right, but later on, after we had time to think about it, we determined we would like to put them on the tails of the aircraft just below the spade. That is where they were moved to, and that is where they are today.

An interesting thing is that another one of the F-14s came by the ship right after we had landed, and they happened to accidently salvo all of their flares all at once. They were going about four to five hundred miles an hour around the ship, coming in for their landing, so it created a string of flares about half a mile long. It was really something to see, and it looked really great. Everyone loved watching that.

One thing I would like to say is that I feel that anybody in my squadron could do the same thing that I did. It was simply me being in the right place at the right time with the right results. I am sure that Dave, the Skipper, and Jim Anderson all feel the same way. We are all trained the same, we all do the same flying, we all fly the same aircraft. There is no difference between the aircraft in the squadron. They are all maintained the same, they are all painted the same, they are all flown the same, they all have the same equipment in them. None are any better or worse than the others, and I think the maintenance in VF-41 is fantastic. We have a lot of good "up" aircraft available to us at all times. That's probably why we won the Clifton Award, the Battle E, and the Safety S for 1981.

In Summary....

The Su-22 killers. Left to right are Lt. Dave Venlet, Cdr. Hank Kleemann, Lt. Larry Muczynski, and Lt. Jim Anderson
(VF-41)

F-14 TOMCAT TECHNICAL DATA

PERFORMANCE:

Maximum Speed	Mach 2.34
Cruise Speed	400-555 Knots
Approach Speed	120 Knots
Minimum Field Take Off Distance	1,000 Feet
Minimum Field Landing Distance	2,000 Feet
Service Ceiling	60,000 Feet
Effective Combat Wing Loading	40-50 PSF
Range	2,000 Miles

WEIGHTS:

Empty	38,000 Pounds
Fighter T.O. with 4 Sparrows	56,000 Pounds
Fighter T.O. with 6 Phoenix	69,000 Pounds
Max Gross Weight	72,000 Pounds
Max External Stores	14,500 Pounds

ENGINES:

2 Pratt & Whitney TF 30-P-412A Turbofans

Max Thrust (each)	20,900 Pounds
Internal Fuel	16,200 Pounds

MISSILES:

TYPE	LENGTH	DIAMETER	FIN SPAN	WEIGHT
AIM-7E Sparrow	143.71″	7.87″	39.37″/32.28″	441 Pounds
AIM-9H Sidewinder	113″	5″	15″/25″	190 Pounds
AIM-9L Sidewinder	113″	5″	22″/25″	190 Pounds
AIM-54A Phoenix	155.9″	15″	36″	985 Pounds

DIMENSIONS

MEASUREMENT	ACTUAL	1/72nd SCALE	1/48th SCALE	1/32nd SCALE
Wingspan (Extended)	64' 1.5"	10.69"	16.03"	24.05"
Wingspan (Swept)	38' 1.9"	6.36"	9.54"	14.31"
Wingspan (Overswept)	32' 8.5"	5.45"	8.18"	12.27"
Length	61' 11.9"	10.33"	15.50"	23.25"
Dist. between Vertical Tails at Tips	10' 8"	1.78"	2.67"	4.00"
Track, Main Landing Gear	16' 5"	2.74"	4.10"	6.16"
Horizontal Tail Span	33' 3.5"	5.55"	8.32"	12.48"
Height	16' 0"	2.67"	4.00"	6.00"

Actual dimensions supplied by U.S. Navy

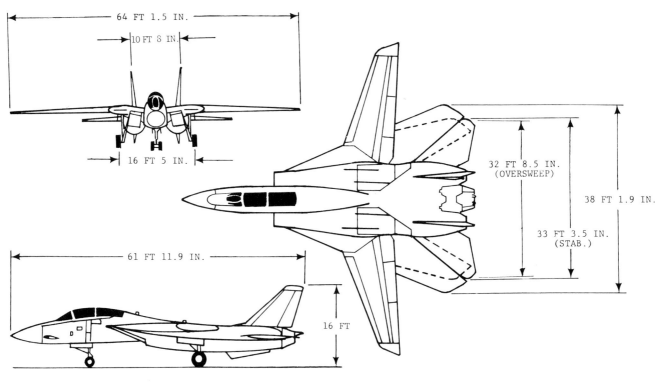

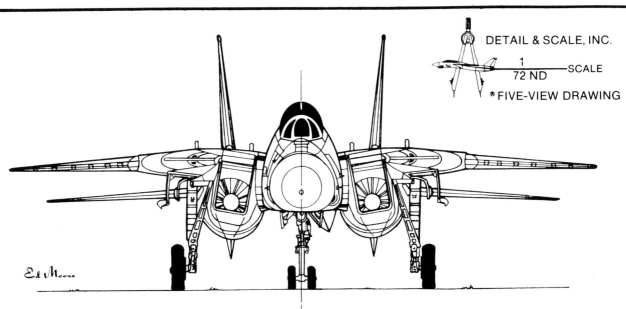

DETAIL & SCALE, INC.

$\frac{1}{72\text{ ND}}$ SCALE

® FIVE-VIEW DRAWING

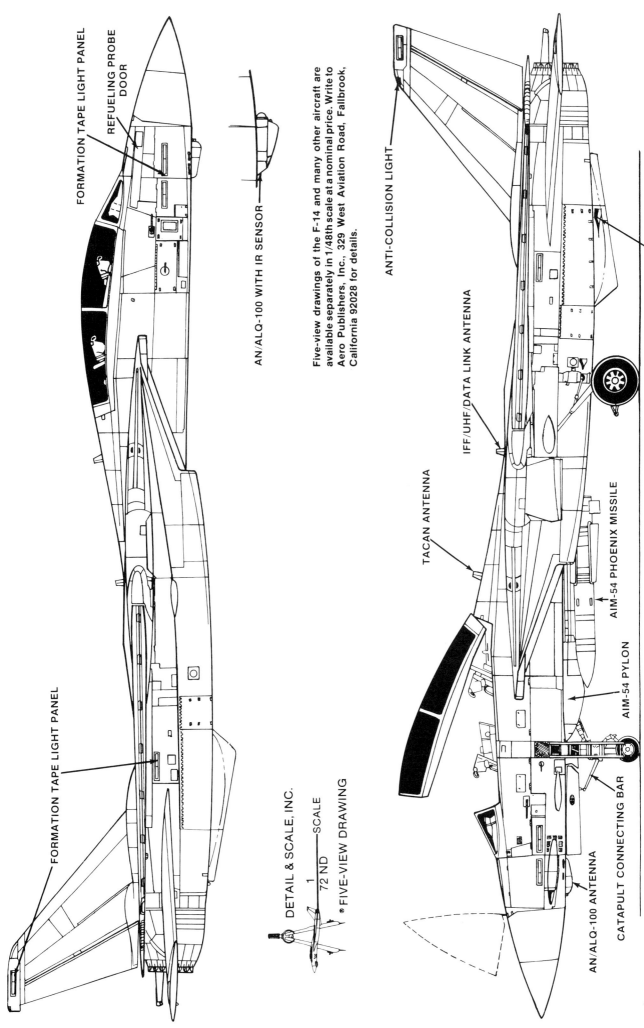

FORMATION TAPE LIGHT PANEL

REFUELING PROBE DOOR

FORMATION TAPE LIGHT PANEL

AN/ALQ-100 WITH IR SENSOR

Five-view drawings of the F-14 and many other aircraft are available separately in 1/48th scale at a nominal price. Write to Aero Publishers, Inc., 329 West Aviation Road, Fallbrook, California 92028 for details.

DETAIL & SCALE, INC.

1
72 ND SCALE

® FIVE-VIEW DRAWING

ANTI-COLLISION LIGHT

OIL COOLER INTAKE (LEFT SIDE OF EACH STRAKE ONLY)

IFF/UHF/DATA LINK ANTENNA

TACAN ANTENNA

AIM-54 PHOENIX MISSILE

AIM-54 PYLON

CATAPULT CONNECTING BAR

AN/ALQ-100 ANTENNA

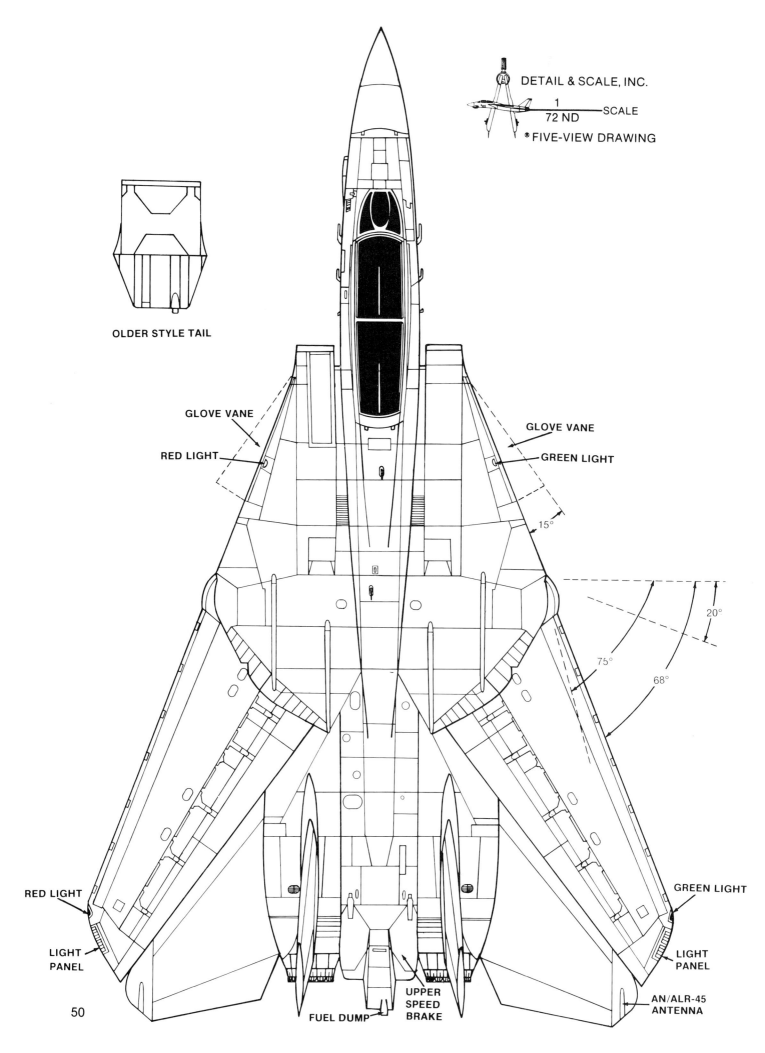

DETAIL & SCALE, INC.

$\frac{1}{72\,ND}$ ─── SCALE

® FIVE-VIEW DRAWING

OLDER STYLE TAIL

GLOVE VANE

RED LIGHT

GLOVE VANE

GREEN LIGHT

15°

20°

75°

68°

RED LIGHT

GREEN LIGHT

LIGHT PANEL

LIGHT PANEL

AN/ALR-45 ANTENNA

FUEL DUMP

UPPER SPEED BRAKE

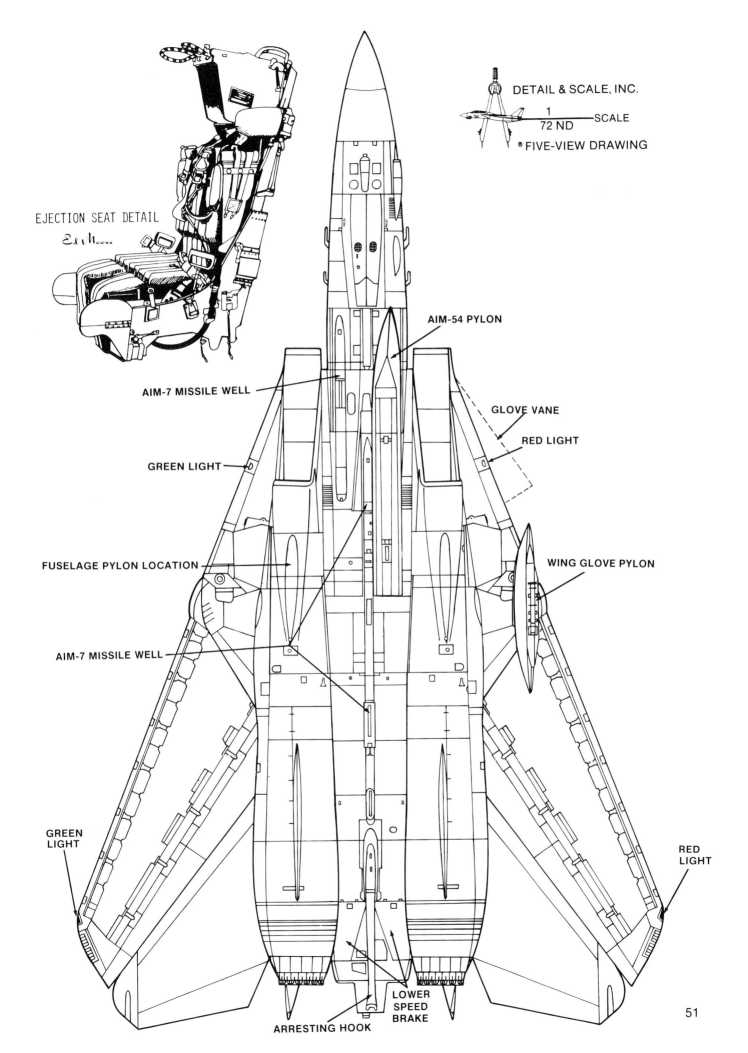

EJECTION SEAT DETAIL
Ed Moore

DETAIL & SCALE, INC.
1
72 ND ——— SCALE
® FIVE-VIEW DRAWING

AIM-54 PYLON

AIM-7 MISSILE WELL

GLOVE VANE

RED LIGHT

GREEN LIGHT

FUSELAGE PYLON LOCATION

WING GLOVE PYLON

AIM-7 MISSILE WELL

GREEN LIGHT

RED LIGHT

LOWER SPEED BRAKE

ARRESTING HOOK

51

THE CLAWS OF THE CAT

An F-14 of VF-32 shown armed with six AIM-54 Phoenix missiles. **(Grumman)**

The Tomcat's job is fleet defense. To perform this mission, it must not only maintain air superiority over enemy aircraft, it must also be able to defend against the threat of surface and air launched missiles such as those that took their toll against British ships during the fight for the Falkland Islands. In the case of air-launched missiles, the best answer is to destroy the carrier aircraft before the missile is launched.

Although bombs were tried on the F-14 during its development, an almost absurd notion, the Tomcat remains strictly an air-to-air machine, and it carries a more formidable array of weapons to perform this mission than any other aircraft in the world. A six-barrel Vulcan cannon is mounted internally (see page 36), as its deletion on the F-14's predecessor, the F-4 Phantom, proved unwise even in the day of missiles. Up to four AIM-9 Sidewinders, and six AIM-7 Sparrows can be carried. But what sets the F-14 apart from all other fighters is the AIM-54 Phoenix. It is this missile, coupled with the AWG-9 weapons system, that gives the Tomcat its capability to attack up to six aircraft at once at ranges in excess of one-hundred miles. The Phoenix can be used against small missiles skimming a few feet above the water, or large MiG-25 Foxbats flying in excess of 100,000 feet of altitude. But one of the best attributes of the Phoenix is its launch-and-leave capability. Unlike semi-active radar homing missiles like the Sparrow, the Phoenix has active homing in the terminal phase of its flight. This means that the aircraft is free to "leave" the missile and do other important things like maneuver against other enemy aircraft. With the semi-active system, the launching aircraft must keep its radar locked on the target aircraft in order to "illuminate" it for the missile. This leaves the launching aircraft more vulnerable to other enemy aircraft, and prevents it from turning its attention to another target.

With the Vulcan cannon, and the Sidewinder, Sparrow, and Phoenix missiles, the Tomcat remains the best armed air-to-air aircraft in the world, and is likely to remain so for some time to come.

Simultaneous Six Target Attack

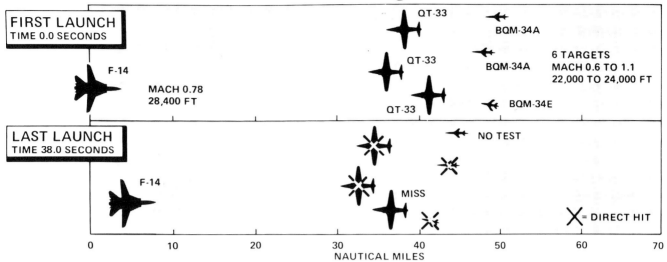

This launch mission objective was to demonstrate the AWG-9 and Phoenix missile capability to track and attack six targets simultaneously. Six Phoenix were launched in rapid sequence against a six target drone raid that was being tracked by the AWG-9 in its unique track-while-scan (TWS) operating mode. At the time of first launch, the fighter was at 28,400 feet altitude and Mach 0.78. The targets were flying toward the fighter in two rows of three at approximately 23,000 feet altitude and at various speeds. Three unaugmented drone QT-33s were in the forward row and two BQM-34As and one BQM-34E in the rear row, all augmented to 10 square meters. Launch ranges varied from 31 to 50 nautical miles. All missiles were launched within 38 seconds and flight times of the four successful launches were between 78 and 107 seconds. Of the six missiles launched, four were direct hits, one was a no test, and one was a miss. The miss was caused by a missile antenna control loop failure. The no test score was due to a loss of target augmentation which caused the missile and AWG-9 to lose track on the target. This condition, which cannot occur in a real attack, is a consequence of simulating hostile targets with remote-controlled drones.

Fighter Attack with Screening Noise Jammer

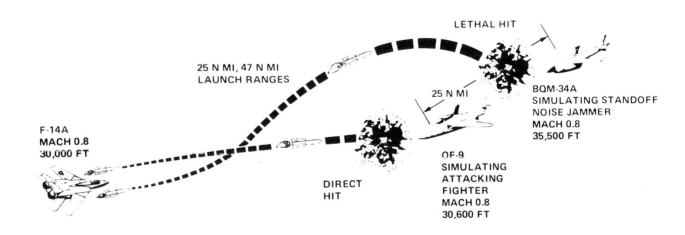

This test simulated an enemy raid employing electronic countermeasures. The raid consisted of a QF-9 target drone flying an attack course at Mach 0.8 followed by a BQM-34A drone equipped with a jammer to cover the approach of the attacking fighter. While only one fighter target was used in this particular mission, a reasonable expectation would be that several fighters and fighter-bombers would be present in a real raid. The F-14 detected the fighter target and its screening jammer at long range. The first Phoenix missile was launched at a range of 25 nautical miles and scored a direct hit. Nine seconds after launch of the first missile, the second Phoenix was launched at the jammer, which was 47 nautical miles away. It scored a hit by passing the jamming drone well within the Phoenix warhead's large lethal radius.

High Altitude, High Speed Target

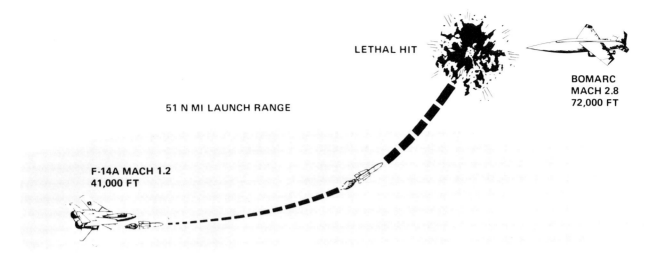

This launch mission demonstrated the ability of Phoenix to destroy sophisticated high altitude, high speed targets. Such targets are capable of flying at speeds and altitudes that make them essentially immune to any other weapon. A BOMARC missile drone was augmented to simulate the radar cross section of an actual aircraft and was flown at Mach 2.8 at 72,000 feet altitude. A single Phoenix was launched from an F-14 51 nautical miles away, flying straight and level at Mach 1.2. The missile climbed more than 5 nautical miles vertically and scored a lethal hit on the BOMARC. Phoenix has performed such interceptions four times, including a direct hit and a warhead kill.

Long Range Capability

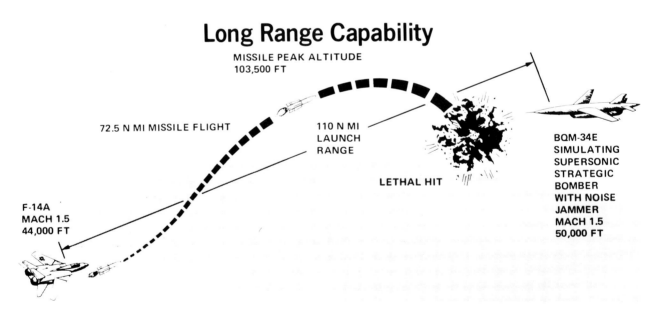

Another air threat is the supersonic strategic bomber. This bomber was simulated by a BQM-34E supersonic target drone augmented to represent the radar cross section of the bomber. As would be expected in a real attack, the target was using an on-off blinking noise jammer to confuse radar defenses. The target flew toward the F-14 at an altitude of 50,000 feet and a speed of Mach 1.5. The F-14 began tracking the approaching bomber with the AWG-9 system in the track-while-scan mode at 132 nautical miles and launched a single Phoenix at 110 nautical miles. During flight, the Phoenix reached a high point in its trajectory of 103,500 feet. No other known air-to-air missile has ever flown so far and high and intercepted its target.

Cruise Missile Target

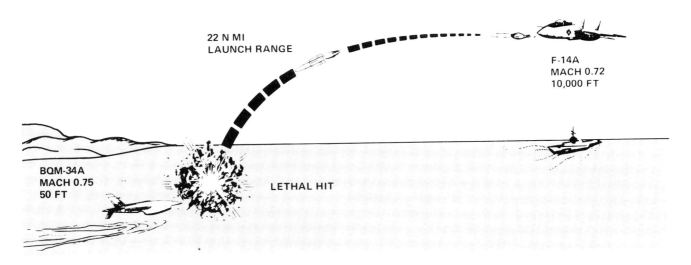

Cruise missiles are a serious threat to surface ships. These weapons, which are launched from aircraft, surface ships, or submarines, can fly just above the surface of the water to avoid radar detection and interception by defensive weapons. Cruise missile vulnerability to Phoenix-armed F-14s has been demonstrated in many low altitude target attack missions. For example, the mission illustrated was a Phoenix shootdown attack on a very small simulated cruise missile target, a BQM-34A drone under remote operator control, which was flying 50 feet above the surface of the sea on a simulated anti-ship cruise missile attack. One Phoenix missile was launched from an F-14 at an altitude of 10,000 feet and a range of 22 nautical miles. The missile scored a lethal hit by passing the target within the Phoenix warhead lethal radius and by having the warhead fuze (target detecting device) trigger on the target.

(Drawings and information on pages 53, 54, and 55 are courtesy of Hughes Aircraft.)

Violently Maneuvering Target

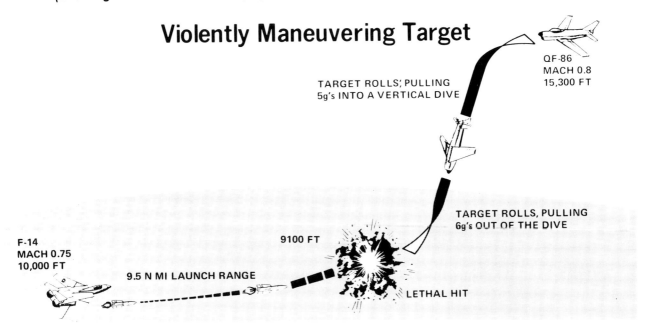

While not intended as a dogfight missile, Phoenix has greater capability against maneuvering targets than any other air-to-air missile. For example, in the illustrated launch mission, a QF-86 drone attempted to break AWG-9 and Phoenix track by violently maneuvering in the vertical plane 16 seconds after missile launch. The drone pulled 5g's going into a 6200 foot dive and 6g's coming out. Phoenix scored a lethal hit on the drone just as it pulled out of the dive. In other evasively maneuvering target launches, Phoenix has pulled as many as 16g's to hit the target.

55

AIM-54 PHOENIX

Above left: AIM-54 Phoenix missile on a trailer.
(U.S. Navy)

Above right: Phoenix mounted on a glove pylon with a Sidewinder shoulder mounted above.
(via Munkasy)

Left: Crewmen position the rear pallets which are used for mounting two Phoenix missiles to the rear fuselage stations. *(U.S. Navy)*

Below left: The two forward Phoenix pallets shown hanging from the fuselage. The forward fairings for these pallets are still attached on top. These will be removed and fastened to the front end of the pallets as they are raised into position on the fuselage.
(U.S. Navy)

Below right: Forward pallets from behind, shown attached to the forward fuselage on either side of the front of the middle Sparrow bay. *(U.S. Navy)*

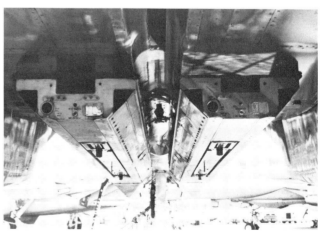

AIM-9 SIDEWINDER

Sidewinder missiles shown in storage. The two larger missiles at the lower right are bodies for AIM-7 Sparrows. **(U.S. Navy)**

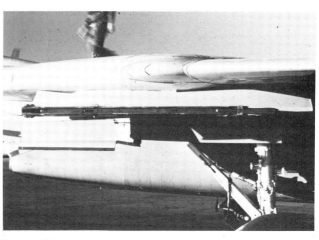

Single Sidewinder launch rail shown mounted on the left glove pylon.

Two views of the dual Sidewinder launch rail combination on the left glove station. Note that one rail is shoulder mounted, while the other is below the pylon.

Sidewinder launch rail shown in position with an AIM-54 Phoenix pylon attached on the right glove station. AIM-9s are carried only on the glove stations, but various combinations are used with the Phoenix, Sparrow, and other Sidewinder missiles.

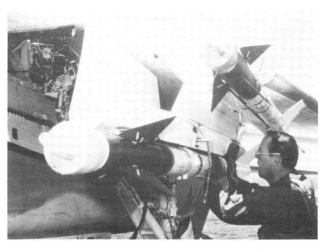

A pilot checks his Sidewinders prior to a flight: Note the protective caps over the missile seeker heads. **(U.S. Navy)**

AIM-7 SPARROW

A Sparrow missile can be seen on this F-14 under the glove pylon. Note the Sidewinder missile shown in combination with the Sparrow. *(Alcock)*

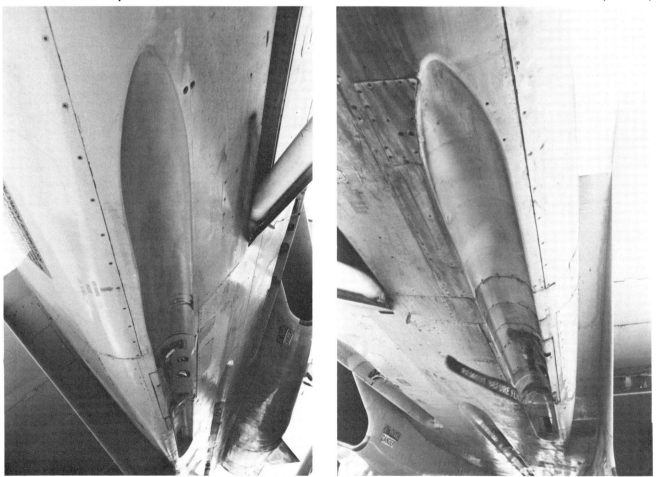

Views of the right and left forward fuselage Sparrow bays. These are similar to the bays on an F-4 Phantom. When Phoenix pallets are carried, these bays are covered.

Above left: Sparrow launch pylon shown on the left glove station. Note the fairing which houses connections for the missile. This fairing is only on the left side of the pylon. On the right glove station, this fairing is on the inside next to the fuselage.

(Munkasy)

Above right: Forward Sparrow bays, and front part of the center bays as seen from behind.

Below left: Center Sparrow bays from the front. Two Sparrows can be carried in these bays, one behind the other.

Below right: Close-up of a portion of the center Sparrow bays showing the mounting brackets and slots for the fins.

MODELER'S SECTION

KIT REVIEWS

When Detail & Scale released the first edition of this book, we finished the kit review section with some "general comments." In these comments we stated that the ultimate 1/48th scale F-14 kit had not been released at that time. We also stated that we would like to see an F-14 kit in 1/32nd scale. Since that time, the ultimate 1/48th scale F-14 has been released by Monogram, and not one, but two 1/32nd F-14s have been released. Additionally, a new 1/144th scale model by LS has appeared, and it is better than the two previous ones. We are happy to add these kits to our reviews, and we can now say that excellent kits of the F-14 exist in all popular scales from 1/144th through 1/32nd.

1/144th SCALE KITS

Crown 1/144th Scale F-14, Kit Number 440-100, and Revell 1/144th Scale F-14, Kit Number 1044.

Judging from the above title, it may sound like we are reviewing two kits at once, but the Revell kit is simply the Crown model reboxed with new decals. Before the LS kit was released, the Crown kit was the better of the two other 1/144th scale F-14s. But it did have its problems. While the overall shape and outline

Combination photo showing the Crown 1/144th scale model (left), the Otaki 1/144th scale kit (right), and the Mania 1/100th scale kit (center).

was "basically correct," some details were lacking, or, if present, were incorrect. For example, the model had what appeared to be two gun muzzles rather than the rear fairing simply being a bulge over the gun's rotating mechanism. The tips of the vertical stabilizers were too rounded, and were identical to each other rather than being different as on the actual aircraft. In short, all edges appear to be too rounded.

The Sparrow missiles only vaguely resembled the real thing, and small parts were generally too thick, lacked detail, and were inaccurate.

This model may be a good beginner's kit, but really isn't for the serious modeler. Only the Revell version is now available.

Otaki 1/144th Scale F-14, Kit Number OT2-19

If the Crown/Revell kit is poor, this model is worse. It is inaccurate in dimensions and proportions. Its shape is so bad that it just doesn't look like an F-14. Detail is lacking for the most part, and small pieces are very crude. The intakes are plugged, the canopy is too thick, and the hump or fairing behind the cockpit is too large. The one good feature of the kit is its decals which are above average for a 1/144th scale fighter. Without using a lot of space for this model, suffice it to say that if you want to build a Tomcat in 1/144th scale, use the LS kit reviewed below. This kit just isn't in the same class as some of the beautiful Otaki models that are available in 1/48th scale.

LS 1/144th Scale F-14, Kit Number J4

This kit is easily the best in this small scale, and while not perfect, it is generally accurate in shape and dimensions. The small parts are much better than in the other two kits, and the Sparrow missiles, in particular, are the only ones in this scale that even resemble the real thing. Don't be misled by the box art which shows six Phoenix and two Sidewinders as armament. The kit comes with only four Sparrows. The box art also shows the VF-2 markings on the inside of the ventral fins, when they are only on the outside. Without going into much detail (there really isn't much to go into in a kit this size!), suffice it to say that this is the best F-14 kit in 1/144th scale, and we recommend this kit.

Box art for the LS 1/144th scale kit.

1/100th SCALE KIT

Mania 1/100th Scale F-14, Kit Number 009-300

This kit makes up into an attractive and accurate model of one of the early F-14s. It has the beaver tail like the early aircraft, and has the shorter gun muzzle. Parts fit together quite well, and scribing is nice. Detail is somewhat sparse as is the case with most kits done in this small scale. Decals are available for VF-124 and the number 5 preproduction aircraft. For VF-124, the stripes for the wing and horizontal tail are missing, and the decals have a yellow film that is quite noticeable if not trimmed away or painted over. Construction is straight forward, and the wings operate between the forward and swept positions. However the overswept position cannot be obtained without plastic surgery to modify the kit. Four Sparrow missiles are included, but no Sidewinders or Phoenix missiles are present. The wing glove pylon is likewise omitted. But this is a good model for this scale, and it will fit well into any 1/100th scale collection. We recommend this model.

Mania 1/100th scale F-14.

1/72nd SCALE KITS

Monogram 1/72nd Scale F-14, Kit Number 5992

This was the first kit ever released of the Tomcat. It does not represent a production, or even a preproduction aircraft, but was modeled after the full scale mock-up. Therefore it is quite dated, and requires extensive modification in order to represent even one of the first prototypes. An article on page 88 of IPMS Quarterly, Volume 7, Number 3 explains in detail how to modify this kit to make it accurate. We highly recommend that any modeler who desires to build this kit should consult this article. Decals are ficticious, and must be replaced with others. Due to this kit's age, and because it represents a mock-up of the real thing rather than an actual aircraft, this kit cannot be very highly recommended.

Matchbox 1/72nd Scale F-14, Kit Number PK 406, and AMT Kit Number 7128

Again, we are not reviewing two different kits. The AMT kit is the Matchbox kit reboxed, and even the decals are for the same markings.

The kit represents a preproduction aircraft. However, the gun muzzle appears to be of the type fitted to production aircraft. Preproduction aircraft featured larger and differently shaped wing fences and a differently contoured fixed portion of the wing at the boundary between the fixed and moveable parts. These preproduction features are represented in this kit.

The kit contains 57 parts molded in multicolored plastic. One of these colors is black which is harder to cover with white and light gull gray paint. Phoenix and Sparrow missiles are provided. Overall dimensions seem pretty close to scale, perhaps being a bit on the short side. As is typical with Matchbox, panel lines are extremely heavy and are bigger than on the real thing. Scaled up they could be used for trench warfare! It could be argued that this allows for more sanding without removing the panel lines, but this would be true only for a modeler who was very ham-handed with sandpaper.

Several parts fit poorly, most noteworthy, parts 19 and 20. A good bit of filling and sanding is required here. Detail is lacking in the cockpit to include the control column. The ventral strakes should be repositioned forward as they are not properly located on the model. Consult the drawings in this book for proper location. The air bleed-off vents are missing completely, and should be added on top of the wing.

The sample kit was built to represent an early development aircraft. Primary colors are gull gray, white, and red. Microscale decals were used. With some extra effort this kit can be made into an attractive model.

Airfix 1/72nd Scale F-14, Kit Number 5013, USAirfix Kit Number 50060, and MPC Kit Number 4404

The Airfix kit (and the subsequent re-releases by USAirfix and MPC) is somewhat dated as it has the older style tail shape between the engines, and the shorter gun muzzle fairing. But it also has options not available in other kits. These include speed brakes that can be displayed in the open position, and a refueling probe that can be displayed open. Also, it is the only kit in 1/72nd scale that has a control column in the front cockpit! In our opinion, this kit has the best cockpit detail of any 1/72nd kit even though more can be added. For example, the pedestal and control handle in the center of the rear cockpit is missing entirely, and must be added from spare parts. Instrument panels are nicely scribed. However, only one throttle is in the front cockpit, so another must be added. This is best done by removing the one in the kit and replacing it with two smaller, more accurate ones.

Six Phoenix and four Sparrow missiles are included, but there are no Sidewinders or launch rails for them, so these must be added from another kit. The small ALQ-100 antenna is provided to go under the nose, but not the larger IR sensor. The forward nose gear doors come as one piece for each side, and must be separated into forward and rear sections.

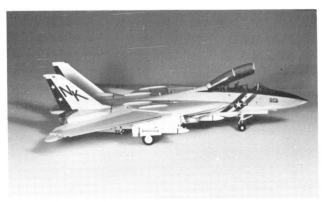

Two views of the Airfix 1/72nd scale Tomcat.

Minicraft F-14 in 1/72nd scale. This kit is easily the best in 1/72nd scale.

Hasegawa 1/72nd Scale F-14, Kit Number JS-134 and Minicraft/Hasegawa Kit Numbers 134 and 1134

We consider this kit to be the best available of the F-14 in 1/72nd scale. The difference between the releases is, as usual, the decals provided. The model is very nicely molded, and the scribing and detailing is very delicate. It fits together very well. The only shortcoming is in the cockpit which is sparse, to say the least. Not even a control column is present. We realize that detailing a cockpit raises tooling costs, but we cannot believe a simple control stick would be very expensive. Likewise, the area behind the front seat under the instruments of the rear cockpit is open. You can see behind the front seat under the instruments to where the NFO's legs would be. Therefore this area must be built up with plastic stock. Likewise, the area behind the rear seat must be built up.

The kit comes with Phoenix, Sparrow, and Side-

This photo shows a comparison of the available 1/72nd scale kits. The Matchbox kit in the center represents an early prototype, the Airfix at left represents an early production aircraft with the older tail, and the Minicraft kit at right is how the Tomcat appears today.

winder missiles, and is the only kit in this scale that has all three types. The IR sensor and ALQ-100 antenna combination is available in the kit as is the ALQ-100 antenna alone, so the modeler has the choice to use either part to represent the particular installation on the aircraft he is modeling.

Molding is very delicate with raised panel lines. More noticeable detail like the flying surfaces and afterburner detail is recessed. The canopy and windscreen are very thin and clear. Shape, proportions and dimensions are good. The landing gear struts, doors, and wheels are all excellent. All wheel wells are enclosed and have some detailing.

With some detailing added in the cockpit, this kit builds up into a nice looking and accurate model. We recommend this kit as the best in 1/72nd scale.

Monogram Snap-Tite 1/72nd Scale F-14, Snap-Tite Kit Number 1104

This kit is primarily designed for the young or the beginning modeler. While it lacks the detail of some other 1/72nd scale kits, it is quite good for the snap-together type of kit. It is generally accurate, and we would rate it above the Matchbox/AMT and earlier Monogram 1/72nd scale kits. We will not dwell on this kit, but we highly recommend it for the younger and less experienced modeler.

Monogram's Snap-Tite F-14 model.

1/48th SCALE KITS

Revell 1/48th Scale F-14, Kit Number H-291

The Revell kit represents a production aircraft and is molded in light gray plastic. It has 64 parts plus Phoenix, Sparrow, and Sidewinder missiles. Scribing is the raised type, but the molding is not as sharp as it should be. There were quite a few sink marks in the sample model, particularily in the landing gear.

Fit is generally good, but filling and sanding is required to fill seams.

Certain modifications are required to correct the shape of some parts. The Sidewinder launch rails are incorrect at the rear, and the forward fins of the Sidewinder missiles are of the type used on the AIM-9J.

This is a USAF version which is not used on the F-14.

A word of caution about the instructions. The Phoenix missile pylons (parts 69 and 70) have their numbers transposed, and should be reversed from what is on the instruction sheet.

Interior detail is sparse, and does not even include a control stick. It is hard to believe this would be omitted in a 1/48th scale kit. Surface scribing is likewise sparse, and the vents around the cannon are not even represented. Much scribing and detail visible on the box art is not present on the kit. Indeed, for the most part, the kit in the box and the model in the box art are not the same.

Fujimi 1/48th Scale F-14, Kit Number 5A-29

This is basically a good kit, but it certainly is not without its shortcomings. Molding is sharp, and scribing and detailing is good. The cockpit needs some work, again requiring plastic stock to close in the area between the two cockpits. There is no pedestal and control handle in the NFO's cockpit.

The radome can be displayed in the open position, and the basics for the radar are included. Phoenix, Sparrow, and Sidewinder missiles are provided, but the Sidewinders are really bad and simply cannot be used.

The fit between the wings where they intermesh is way off. We had to remove most of this part of the wing in order to get it to fit, thus making the wings inoperable. Another bad place is the horizontal stabilizer. The tips are totally incorrect in shape and are missing the small ECM antennas. We would recommend using our 1/48th scale drawings in order to get the correct shape.

Another area where this kit is in error is inside the air intakes. The top part extends down too far into the intake, and it would take a great deal of work to correct this.

On the plus side, molding is sharp, and details,

Revell F-14 in 1/48th scale.

dimensions and proportions are generally accurate. But the Monogram kit is even better, and with the high price of this kit, the Monogram kit comes out on top. However, if you already have this kit, it can be built into an impressive model with some work and corrections.

Fujimi 1/48th scale Tomcat.

Monogram 1/48th Scale F-14, Kit Number 5803

This is unquestionably the best F-14 kit in 1/48th scale of the F-14, and, in our opinion, the best overall available in any scale.

The model is beautifully molded, exquisitely detailed, and as accurate as plastic can be molded. Anything that could be detailed is detailed. In the cockpits, the instrument panels and consoles are molded in the plastic, and just about every switch seems in place. About the only things missing are the throttle handles, and these are easily added. The seats are masterpieces, and we cannot think of any

better in any 1/48th scale kit. Lines, handles, levers, buckles, belts, and ejection rings are all represented.

Wheels are nicely detailed, struts are delicate and sharp, and landing gear doors are extensively detailed. Wheel wells have lots of hydraulic lines and fittings molded in, and the nose gear well has extra piping to glue in. The nose gear doors are molded in place on the walls of the well, thus insuring that they are positioned at the correct angle.

An open boarding ladder is supplied in the kit, but, strangely enough, does not show up on the instruction sheet. Instruction sheets are one of two consistently poor features in Monogram kits (the other being the decals), and these instructions could definitely be improved upon.

The fit between the top and bottom fuselage halves requires care, and will need some filling and sanding. Another negative point is that the Sparrow missiles are molded as part of the glove pylon, and this makes painting them white on an all gray aircraft a difficult task. Likewise, the stabilators are molded as part of the upper fuselage, and, as a matter of preference, we think it would be better if they had been made as separate pieces. The ventral fins are molded as part of the lower fuselage, and, as a result, the cooling intakes on them are not molded as well as they should be.

Ordnance consists of four Phoenix missiles that are to be mounted under the fuselage, two Sparrows, mounted under the glove pylons as mentioned above, and two beautiful AIM-9L Sidewinders shoulder mounted on the glove pylons.

Decals are not as extensive as they were in the Monogram F-15 and F-4C/D kits, particularly when it

The Monogram F-14 in 1/48th scale is the best model of the Tomcat in this scale.

comes to the smaller stenciling.

This model is excellent, and its shortcomings are relatively minor. We recommend this kit as the best available in 1/48th scale.

1/32nd SCALE KITS

Tamiya 1/32nd F-14, Kit Number 6301

This kit is very large in a number of ways, not the least of which is its price tag. We have seen it advertised from $65.00 to $80.00, and it probably has been offered at a range greater than this. Most prices have been closer to the $80.00 figure, and one would think that you should get a truly superb kit for this price. Many modelers, awed by the size and excellent detailing on some parts of this kit, have called it the ultimate model, and although it is very good, it has some bad shortcomings that are inexcusable in a kit costing over $50.00.

The first area where this kit comes up short is in the cockpit. There is no molding of instruments, knobs, switches, console panels, or scopes. Instead, these are represented by flat, two-dimensional decals. We believe it is almost stealing to charge the price of this kit, and use decals for the instrument panels and consoles. If Monogram can do such a beautiful job engraving their panels and consoles, and if Revell can do such a nice job in their 1/32nd F-14 for a fraction of the price, then why can't Tamiya?

The second shortcoming is the engraved panel lines, some of which are really overdone. Most noticeable of these are some panels on the nose which look more like armor plating bolted or welded on the sides. If scaled up, these would be large, drag-producing panels that protrude out from the skin rather than being flush with other panels.

The third poor area is the decal sheet. Tamiya must think that "NO STEP" is one word. The same is true for "NO LIFT." The yellow in the markings, such as the rescue arrows and VF-84 markings, are way too orange, and really look bad on the model. It is ridiculous to spend up to $80.00 on a model, then have it look like a toy because of badly out-of-color decals.

A fourth area that does not directly affect the model itself is the instruction sheet. Some kits that have found their way into the U.S., have only Japanese instruction sheets. MRC has advised that modelers should check to see that they are getting a kit with the MRC label. MRC imported kits do have English instructions. The English instructions are helpful for such an intricate kit with so many parts.

It may sound like we are being nothing but critical of this kit, and so far we have been, but considering the price, the criticism is justified. We realize that import duties and tariffs raise the price of a kit brought in from another country, but the price of this kit seems completely unjustified.

But this kit is loaded with good points - even great ones that would take many pages to cover. The ejection seats are models in and of themselves, each having about sixteen pieces. With all this detail in the seats, it seems inconsistent to use decals for instruments! The landing gear is like the seats, and consist

The Tamiya F-14 in 1/32nd scale is a beautiful model. But it does have its problems, and is unbelievably expensive.
(Evans)

of numerous parts that build up into the most detailed replica possible of the real thing. Actuating cylinders are given as separate pieces for the doors, which in turn are nicely detailed as are the wheel wells. There is a nice radar, but no hinge for the radome. Tamiya evidently intended for the radome to be completely removed if the radar is to be displayed.

Inside the intakes, the ramps can be positioned in any one of three positions, and at the other end of the engines, the afterburner can, engine grid, and nozzles are beautiful.

Armament consists of four AIM-9H Sidewinders, three AIM-7 Sparrows, and four AIM-54 Phoenix missiles. All are very well done, particularly the Sparrows, which have the appropriate fairings on the sides of the body. If building a Su-22 killer, we recommend replacing the AIM-9Hs with AIM-9Ls from a Minicraft/Hasegawa F-18. Also in the external store category, fuel tanks and pylons are provided for the under-intake positions.

Other goodies include a detailed boarding ladder, optional position canopy, and optional fuselage bladders behind the wing that are chosen based on whether you want the wings in a forward or swept (or moving) position. Additionally, the upper and lower speed brakes may be shown in the open position.

This is a beautiful kit, and we highly recommend it. It is just unfortunate that Tamiya did not do justice to the cockpit, decals, scribing, and instructions. With extra detailing, this kit becomes a masterpiece. Whether it is worth its price is up to the individual modeler and his pocketbook.

Revell 1/32nd F-14, Kit Number 4712

Costing about one-fifth what the Tamiya kit does, this kit also has its share of good and bad points. In early 1980, Revell asked Detail & Scale to provide photos of the cockpits of the F-14 to assist in detailing this model. As a result, Revell did a much better job detailing the instrument panels and consoles than did Tamiya. But Revell's seats are two-piece affairs that don't come close to Tamiya's in regard to detail. Like the Tamiya kit, the Revell kit has very large panel lines, but has none of the protruding panels of the Tamiya kit.

The landing gear struts, wheels, doors, and wells are not as well detailed as Tamiya's, and this is generally true for all of the parts in the kit. But it boils down to getting what you pay for. This Revell kit is nicely detailed, and accurately so, and it is probably adequate for many modelers. You can do a lot of detailing on your own for the difference in price. But we cannot make this decision. Each modeler must make it for himself. Is the extra detail of the Tamiya kit worth it?

The Revell kit is accurate in scale and proportions, and has some nice extras. External fuel tanks are provided, and armament consists of two Sidewinders, two Sparrows, and four Phoenix.

Being accurate, this model builds up into an excellent model. Extra detailing can result in a most impressive replica of the Tomcat. We recommend this kit.

The Revell 1/32nd scale kit can be built into a beautiful model of the F-14. **(Revell)**

WALDRON MODEL PRODUCTS COCKPIT PLACARDS

Since Tamiya left the instrument panels and consoles bare in its 1/32nd scale Tomcat, it is nice to know that Waldron Model Products will be producing some of their excellent cockpit placards for the F-14 in the spring of 1983. These placards build up into super detailed cockpits, and we highly recommend them. We received a pre-production sample of the F-14 placards, and they are just beautiful. If anyone is going to invest the money and time to build a Tamiya (or Revell for that matter) F-14 kit in 1/32nd scale, these placards are a real must. Further information on these placards and other Waldron Model Products can be obtained by writing to them at 1358 Stephen Way, San Jose, California 95129.

A.I.R. F-14 T-SHIRT

While it is unusual for us to cover a non-modeling product in our Modeler's Section, this T-shirt from A.I.R. and Don Spering seemed worthy of exception. The T-shirt commemorates the downing of the two Su-22s by F-14s of VF-41. It depicts F-14s flying over the USS NIMITZ with an exploding Su-22 in front of them. In the explosion are the letters "VMAK!" which are the last name initials of the four U.S. crewmen involved in the incident. The shirt reads, "Anytime Baby, Compliments of the Black Aces, Nimitz-2, Libya-0." Shirts come in blue or yellow, and small, medium, large, or extra large. They are $7.00 each plus $1.00 postage and handling for the first shirt, and 50¢ for each shirt thereafter. They can only be ordered from, Air Hobbies & Crafts, Rt. 38 Hollyedge Shopping Center, Mt. Holly, New Jersey 08060. Be sure to state color and size.

DECAL SUMMARY

Note: It is impossible to completely review decals unless the reviewer has actually used the decals on a model to see how they fit. Additionally, markings on a given aircraft can be changed from time to time, so it is possible that the decals may be accurate for one point in time and not another. Therefore, this section is more of a listing of decals available than a review. Review comments are made only in regard to fit when we have actually used the decals or as to accuracy when the evidence clearly indicated an error.

1/144th Scale Kit

LS Kit Number J4: Contains markings for an F-14A of VF-2, with NK tail codes and a nose number 201. Minimal markings only are provided. The aircraft is painted in the gray over white scheme.

Crown Kit Number 440-100: Provides only four national insignia and two NAVY markings for the fuselage sides.

Otaki Kit Number OT2-19: Provides markings for an F-14A, 158620, of VF-124. Tail code NJ, nose number 401, gray over white scheme.

Revell Kit Number 1044: Provides markings for an F-14A of VF-32, "Swordsmen," in a gray over white scheme.

1/100th Scale Kits

Mania Kit Number 009-300: Provides markings for the number 5 preproduction aircraft, and an F-14A of VF-124 with no BuNo. Tail code is NJ in a gray over white scheme.

1/72nd Scale Kits

AMT Kit Number 7128: Provides markings for three aircraft.
- F-14A, 159025, VF-142, tail code AJ, gray over white scheme
- F-14A, 159020, VF-2, tail code NK, gray over white scheme.
- F-14A, 159022, VF-32, tail code AB, USS John F. Kennedy, gray over white scheme

Airfix Kit Number 5013: Contains markings for two aircraft.
- F-14A, 158627, VF-1, "Wolfpack," tail code NK, gray over white scheme
- F-14A, 158629, VF-2, tail code NK, USS Enterprise, gray over white scheme

USAirfix Kit Number 50060: Provides markings for an F-14A, 159344, VF-143, "Pukin Dogs," tail code AE, CAG aircraft, USS America, gray over white scheme

MPC Kit Number 4404: Provides marking for same aircraft as the USAirfix kit above.

Minicraft/Hasegawa Kit Number 134: Contains markings for two aircraft in the gray over white scheme.
- F-14A, 159461, VF-1, Wolfpack, tail code NK
- F-14A, 159861, VF-213, tail code NK

Minicraft/Hasegawa Kit Number 1134: Contains markings for two aircraft.
- F-14A, 159861, VF-213, "Black Lions," tail code NH, gray over white scheme
- F-14A, 159543, VF-142, tail code AE, all gray scheme

Hasegawa Kit Number JS-134: Same as Minicraft/Hasegawa kit number 134 above.

Matchbox Kit Number PK 406: Same as AMT kit number 7128 above.

Monogram Kit Number 5992: Provides markings for an F-14A of VF-83, code NK. These markings are ficticious.

Monogram Snap-Tite Kit Number 1104: Contains markings for an F-14A of VF-111, "Sundowners" in an all gray scheme with sharkmouth.

1/48th Scale Kits

Monogram Kit Number 5803: Provides markings for an F-14A, 159449, VF-142, tail code AE from the USS America in a gray over white scheme.

Revell Kit Number H-291: Provides markings for an F-14A, 160382, of VF-84, "Jolly Rogers," tail code AJ, from the USS Nimitz, in a gray over white scheme.

Fujimi Kit Number 5A-29: Provides markings for two aircraft.
- F-14A, 159636, VF-211, tail code NG, USS Constellation, CAG aircraft, gray over white scheme
- F-14A, 159858, VF-114, tail code NH, USS Kitty Hawk, gray over white scheme

1/32nd Scale Kits

Revell Kit Number 4712: Provides markings for an F-14A, 158993, VF-1 "Wolfpack," tail code NK, USS Enterprise in a gray over white scheme.

Tamiya Kit Number 6301: Contains markings for three aircraft.
- F-14A, 158630, VF-211, tail code NG, USS Constellation, CAG aircraft, gray over white scheme
- F-14A, 160393, VF-84, "Jolly Rogers," tail code AJ, USS Nimitz, CAG aircraft, gray over white scheme
- F-14A, 3-863, Imperial Iranian Air Force, Iranian camouflage scheme

1/144th Scale Sheets

Microscale Sheet Number 14-119: Markings for four F-14s in the gray over white scheme are provided.
- F-14A, 158627, VF-1, "Wolfpack," tail code NK
- F-14A, 158629, VF-2, tail code NK
- F-14A, 157983, Naval Missile Center
- F-14A, 158620, VF-124, tail code NJ

Microscale Sheet Number 14-171: Markings for three F-14s in the gray over white scheme are provided.
- F-14A, 159344, VF-143, tail code AE, CAG aircraft, USS America
- F-14A, 159616, VF-124, tail code NJ, bicentennial scheme
- F-14A, 159014, VF-32, "Swordsmen," USS John F. Kennedy

Note: Both of these sheets are 1/72nd scale sheets reduced down 50%. While this is satisfactory for some small decals, it doesn't work when the decal is supposed to fit over an entire part of the aircraft such as a vertical stabilizer, rudder, or ventral fin. Likewise, it is not always satisfactory when the decal fits over a curved surface.

Sizing a decal up or down in scale assumes that the models in the different scales are exactly proportioned. Unfortunately this is not the case. We tried these decals on all of the 1/144th scale models, and they did not properly fit any of them in many cases. The biggest problems were on the ventral fins, with tail and rudder markings fitting poorly. Decals must be designed for a specific model, and not merely sized from other scales, if they are to fit properly.

1/72nd Scale Sheets

Detail & Scale Sheet Number DS-0272, F-14, Su-22 Killers: Provides markings for two F-14s in overall gray.
- F-14, 160403, VF-41, "Black Aces," USS Nimitz, tail code AJ
- F-14, 160390, VF-41, "Black Aces," USS Nimitz, tail code AJ

Note: These are the two F-14s that shot down the Su-22s as described in this book. These sheets were carefully researched with the help of VF-41. Markings are provided to build the aircraft as they appeared during the engagement and also after the engagement when kill markings were added, crew names were changed, and the nose number on 160403 was changed from 102 to 101. Small stencils that are different from those provided on any other decal sheet are provided. The instruction sheet is the largest ever included with a decal sheet, measuring 11 x 14 inches, printed on both sizes, and includes 18 photographs and numerous drawings.

Hasegawa Sheet Number HD 72-09: Provides markings for five aircraft.
- F-14A, 159636, VF-211, tail code NG, CAG aircraft
- F-14A, 159628, VF-211, tail code NG
- F-14A, 159620, VF-211, tail code NG
- F-14A, 160667, VF-51, tail code NL
- F-14A, 160675, VF-51, tail code NL

Hasegawa Sheet Number HD 72-010: Provides markings for five aircraft.
- F-14A, 159631, VF-24, tail code NG, CAG aircraft
- F-14A, 159449, VF-142, tail code AE, low visibility markings
- F-14A, 159445, VF-142, tail code AE, USS America
- F-14A, 160441, VF-101, tail code AD
- F-14A, 158620, VF-101, tail code AD

Microscale Sheet Number 72-119: Same as Microscale sheet number 14-119.

Microscale Sheet Number 72-171: Same as Microscale sheet number 14-171.

Note: The art for these sheets was designed for 1/72nd scale models, and therefore the fit is much better than that of the 1/144th scale sheets.

Microscale Sheet Number 72-191, Oceana Tomcats: Contains markings for three F-14s.
- F-14A, 159017, VF-14, tail code AB, low visibility markings
- F-14A, 160381, VF-41, tail code AJ, USS Nimitz, gray over white scheme
- F-14A, 160380, VF-84, "Jolly Rogers" tail code AJ, gray over white scheme

Microscale Sheet Number 72-192, Miramar Tomcats: Provides markings for three aircraft.
- F-14A, 159859, VF-114, "Aardvarks," tail code NH, USS Kitty Hawk, gray over white
- F-14A, 159634, VF-211, tail code NG, USS Constellation, gray over white scheme
- F-14A, 159859, VF-213, tail code NH, gray over white scheme

Microscale Sheet Number 72-248: This sheet provides stenciling and data for F-14s. A word of caution is in order in that these stencils are based on what was supposed to be applied to F-14s in the gray over white scheme. However, this stenciling differs considerably from aircraft to aircraft, and is quite different on the most recent all gray subdued schemes. A good reference on the aircraft being modeled should be consulted before using these decals.

Microscale Sheet Number 72-296: Provides markings for three aircraft.
- F-14A, 160665, VF-51, tail code NL, gray over white scheme
- F-14A, 159631, VF-24, tail code NL, CAG aircraft, gray over white scheme
- F-14A, 160666, VF-111, "Sundowners," tail code NL, sharkmouth, gray over white scheme

Microscale Sheet Number 72-337: Contains markings for two F-14As.
- F-14A, 160403, VF-41, USS Nimitz, tail code AJ, all gray scheme
- F-14A, 160390, VF-14, USS Nimitz, all gray scheme.

Notes: This sheet also contains markings for an A-7E as well as an E-2C. The BuNo for the E-2C (161094) is also erroneously given for F-14 160403, and 160403 is not given at all. This error is surprisingly carried forward on the 1/48th scale and 1/32nd scale sheets Microscale released with these markings (sheets 48-118 and 32-45 respectively) even though the E-2C is not even on those sheets. Therefore the proper BuNo for 160403 is not given by Microscale on any of its sheets. Other errors also exist. Lt. Muczynski's name is misspelled, having an "s" between the "c" and "z." Commander Kleemann's name is misspelled, having only one "n." The BuNo and F-14A markings are the wrong size and shape. The first names of the crew of 107 are given. Only the last names were used until the aircraft returned to Oceana, but at that time several other markings were also changed. Additionally Lt. Anderson's rank is incorrectly given as "LTJG." The 07 on the left vertical tail of 107 is the wrong style and slant. All "7s" on 107 are the wrong style. The "RESCUE" arrows are proportioned incorrectly, and have the letters in "RESCUE" written side-by-side rather than one under the other. Yellow rectangle markings are given for the sides of the nose of the aircraft. Neither of these aircraft have such markings. The "BEWARE OF BLAST" markings are wrong in that they have "BEWARE OF" with "BLAST" underneath. These aircraft had "BEWARE" with "OF" underneath and "BLAST" under that. Hoist markings are the wrong color and have no background. They should be yellow on a white background. The "JET INTAKE" markings are wrong. The word "DANGER" is mislocated. The "107" on the right side of 160390 is different from the "107" on the left side. They show them as both being the same. No aircraft numbers are given for the flaps. The national insignia is the wrong size with wrong proportions. Crew names are not provided for 160403 as it appeared at the time of the engagement. The Su-22 "kill' marking is the wrong size and shape. There are no "EVT" or "GWT" markings for either aircraft. The "AN SUGG" marking is missing from the nose doors of 107. The "AJ" markings on the tails are the wrong style. All crew names are in the wrong style of lettering. The instructions show the red turbine stripe going all the way across the top of the aircraft, but it does not. Further, the instructions show no turbine stripe on the sides of the aircraft. The "USS NIMITZ" marking is mislocated on the glove vane. They do not show instructions for all aircraft. Only one side of one aircraft is presented along with a general top view that does not pertain to these particular aircraft. Finally, several small stencils are provided that are not correct for these aircraft. This is because Microscale has a policy of using the same stenciling data over and over again for the same type of aircraft regardless of what is on the actual aircraft. To get this stenciling correct, careful research is required for the specific aircraft involved.

We are able to completely review the decals for these aircraft because we also researched them. Such reviews are not given for other sheets because we have not extensively researched each of the markings presented, and we do not want to present erroneous information. However, the problems on this sheet which are the result of Microscale using the same stenciling data over and over are present on other sheets as well. Modelers are cautioned to carefully research the specific aircraft they are building before using the stenciling. In certain cases, some or all of this stenciling may be appropriate, in other cases it may not.

Microscale Sheet Number 72-350: Provides markings for three aircraft.
- F-14A, 161283, VF-102, tail code AB, USS America, all gray scheme (TARPS aircraft)
- F-14A, 160674, VF-111, tail code NL, USS Kitty Hawk, with sharkmouth subdued markings on an overall gray aircraft
- F-14A, 161142, VF-101 on loan to VF-33, tail code AD, overall gray scheme

Microscale Sheet Number 72-351: Provides markings for three aircraft.
- F-14A, 159435, VF-143, "Pukin Dogs," USS Eisenhower, tail code AG, all gray scheme
- F-14A, 159010, VF-11, no tail code, CAG aircraft, USS John F. Kennedy, all gray scheme
- F-14A, 159422, VF-31, tail code AC, overall gray scheme

1/48th Scale Sheets

Detail & Scale Sheet Number DS-0348: Same as Detail & Scale Sheet Number DS-0272.

Fowler Sheet Number 4806, Sundowners: Provides markings for two aircraft.
- F-14A, 160656, VF-111, tail code NL, CAG aircraft, red sunburst on fin and red sharkmouth, overall gray scheme
- F-14A, 160668, VF-111, tail code NL, gray sunburst and sharkmouth, overall gray scheme

Fowler Sheet Number 4808, Blacktail Tomcats: Provides markings for two aircraft.

- F-14A, 159593, VF-24, tail code NG, CAG aircraft, USS Constellation, overall gray scheme
- F-14A, 159428, VF-33, tail code AB, USS America, overall gray scheme

Note: These two Fowler sheets, along with the 1/32nd scale sheet covered below, are excellent decals. Fowler makes an effort to be accurate, and, as modelers, they are aware of modelers' problems. We recommend Fowler decals, and for more information, write to Fowler Aviation, P.O. Box 148, Sunnymead, California, 92388.

Microscale Sheet Number 48-56: Provides markings for three aircraft.

- F-14A, 159461, VF-1, "Wolfpack," tail code NK, USS Enterprise, gray over white scheme
- F-14A, 159449, VF-142, tail code AE, USS America, gray over white scheme
- F-14A, 159422, VF-14, "Tophatters," tail code AB, USS Kennedy, overall gull gray

Microscale Sheet Number 48-57, Atlantic Tomcats: Provides markings for three aircraft.

- F-14A, 159869, VF-1, "Wolfpack," tail code NK, CAG aircraft, USS Enterprise, gray over white scheme
- F-14A, 160380, VF-84, "Jolly Rogers" tail code AJ, USS Nimitz, gray over white scheme
- F-14A, 158978, VF-213, tail code NK, USS Kitty Hawk, gray over white scheme

Microscale Sheet Number 48-58: Provides data and stenciling. See notes for sheet number 72-248.

Microscale Sheet Number 48-106: Provides markings for two aircraft.

- F-14A, 160665, VF-51, tail code NL, gray over white scheme
- F-14A, 159631, VF-24, tail code NG, USS Constellation, CAG aircraft, gray over white scheme

Microscale Sheet Number 48-118: Provides markings for two F-14s. These two aircraft are the same Su-22 killers as covered on sheet number 72-337 above. The notes on that sheet apply to this sheet.

Microscale Sheet Number 48-122: Contains markings for two aircraft.

- F-14A, 161283, VF-102, tail code AB, USS America, overall gray scheme, TARPS aircraft.
- F-14A, 160674, VF-111, "Sundowners," tail code NL, USS Kitty Hawk, overall gray scheme with subdued
- markings

Microscale Sheet Number 48-123: Provides markings for two aircraft.

- F-14A, 161142, VF-101 on loan to VF-33, tail code AD, USS America, overall gray scheme
- F-14A, 159010, VF-11, no tail code, CAG aircraft, USS Kennedy, overall gray scheme

Microscale Sheet Number 48-124: Provides markings for two aircraft.

- F-14A, 159422, VF-31, tail code AC, overall gray scheme
- F-14A, 159435, VF-143, tail code AG, USS Eisenhower, overall gray scheme

1/32nd Scale Sheets

Fowler Sheet Number 3201, Sundowners: Provides markings for an F-14A, 160656, VF-111, tail code NL, CAG aircraft, overall gray scheme with red sharkmouth and sunburst.

Note: This sheet provides different fin markings, one set for the Revell kit, one set for the Tamiya kit. This is necessary because the kits are slightly different. Here is an example of what we meant by our comments above about Fowler decals. It is also an example of how decals must be fitted to specific kits when the decals cover an entire part. Compare this to our comments on the 1/144th scale sheets.

Microscale Sheet Number 32-45: Provides markings for three aircraft.

- F-14A, 160403, VF-41, tail code AJ, USS Nimitz, overall gray
- F-14A, 160390, VF-41, tail code AJ, USS Nimitz, overall gray
- F-14A, 159344, VF-143, tail code AE, CAG aircraft, USS America, gray over white scheme

Note: The first two aircraft are again the Su-22 killers as covered on sheets 72-337 and 48-118. Notes presented for sheet 72-337 apply to these two aircraft on this sheet.

Microscale Sheet 32-46: Provides markings for two aircraft

- F-14A, 159631, VF-24, tail code NG, CAG aircraft, USS Constellation, gray over white scheme
- F-14A, 159869, VF-123, "Black Lions," tail code NH, USS Kitty Hawk, gray over white scheme

REFERENCE LISTING

Note: Listed here are references on the Tomcat that should prove helpful in providing information and photographs of a different nature and format than what is presented in this publication. With each listing is a brief description of what that reference covers. There are many fine references on the F-14 Tomcat and they all cannot be listed here. The fact that a given reference is not included in this list is not intended to reflect unfavorably on that reference.

1. Stevenson, James Perry, Grumman F-14 "Tomcat", Aero Publishers, Inc., Fallbrook, California, 1975.

This is an excellent book covering the development and technical data of the F-14. The inner workings of the F-14 such as the computers, radars, and electronics are explained in words, photos and drawings.

2. Reed, Arthur, F-14 Tomcat, Charles Scribner's Sons, New York, 1978.

Very good book on the F-14 that explains the development, construction, sale to Iran, and recovery of the F-14 that went overboard off of the USS John F. Kennedy. Interesting reading.

3. Drendel, Lou, F-14 Tomcat in Action, Squadron/Signal Publications, Warren, Michigan, 1977.

This is one of the best "In Action" books that has come out. There are accounts by pilots who have flown the F-14, and many photos compliment the narrative.

4. Grumman F-14 Tomcat, Koku Fan Special Number 83 (Part I) and Number 89 (Part II), Bunrindo Publications, Bunrin-Do Japan.

Typical Koku Fan specials with extensive photographic coverage of a general nature. Best reference for markings that is available. Japanese text.

5. Godfrey, David W. H., "Dogfighter Supreme, The Tomcat," Air Enthusiast International, January 1974.

Comprehensive article on the development of the F-14 with emphasis on design features, power plants and weapon systems.

6. Maguire, Walter, "The Phoenix Factor," Air Combat, Volume 7, Number 2, March 1979, page 20.

Good article on the Phoenix weapons system and how it sets the F-14 apart from all other fighters.

7. Hotz, Robert B., Editor, "F-14 Overhaul Done at Norfolk Facility," Aviation Week & Space Technology, Vol 106, No. 10, March 7, 1977, page 56.

A short but interesting article on the overhaul the F-14 gets after 30 months of service.

8. Robinson, Clarance A. J., "F-14 Demonstrates Agile Aerial Combat Capabilities," Aviation Week & Space Technology, Volume 105, Number 22, November 29, 1976, page 46.

Informative article that includes the author's report after a flight in the F-14 that lasted almost 2 hours. Covers the F-14's air-to-air capabilities very well.

9. Hotz, Robert B., Editor, "F-14A Fighter Performance Upgraded," Aviation Week & Space Technology, Vol 106, No. 5, January 31, 1977.

Short article covering the improvements that have been made to the F-14 to improve its capabilities and reliability.

10. Braybrook, Roy, "F-14 and F-15, The New Wave of Warplanes," Air Enthusiast, Volume 2, Number 3, March 1972, page 115.

Article about these two aircraft in their early developmental stages. Contains some nice color photos of early F-14 prototypes.